Organic C
Down ꓚouth

Deep South Gardening
the Organic Way

by Nellie Neal

B. B. Mackey Books
P. O. Box 475
Wayne, PA 19087
www.mackeybooks.com

Organic Gardening Down South: Deep South Gardening the Organic Way, by Nellie Neal

text © 2008 by Nellie Neal and Betty Mackey

illustrations and photographs © 2008 by Betty Mackey, Tom Mackey, and Nellie Neal. Other art is from the USDA and public domain sources.

ISBN 1-893443-10-8 9781893443105

CIP requested

B. B. Mackey Books, Publisher
P. O. Box 475
Wayne, PA 19087
www.mackeybooks.com
info@mackeybooks.com

Dedication and Thanks

For my big sister, Paula, whose grace belies her power. Yes, she knocked me off the back steps headlong onto a pitchfork and bounced me off the bed to a broken collarbone. But she stood ready to beat up the neighborhood bully for me, too, and still would if the need arose.

I am particularly indebted to the radio listeners and readers who ask the questions that keep me seeking answers. A friend once said to me in disgust, "You wake up in a new world every day." He was right. My garden is new to me every day, and I wish the same for you.

Thanks to Betty Mackey, my editor and publisher, for knowing and sharing your wisdom.

Special thanks to Jeff Lowenfels for explaining and encouraging as only a Wizard can.

CONTENTS

About Nellie Neal

Nellie Neal is a garden writer and radio host who lived outside the Deep South just long enough to find the road home. She is known for sensible gardening advice grown from a lifetime of experience and education. She grew up in north Louisiana, graduated from LSU where she studied English and Horticulture. Home is Jackson, Mississippi, with strong ties to gardens in New Orleans and Baton Rouge, Louisiana. Known for a contagious style and super-practical garden advice, her regular columns appear in newspapers, magazines, and online. She is the owner of Garden-Mama, Inc., and its website, gardenmama.com, G2C Publications, and a quarterly newsletter, *Garden Mama News and Advice*.

Author:

The Garden Primer, Loose Dirt Publishing, Florence, MS, 1999.

Questions and Answers for Deep South Gardeners, B. B. Mackey Books, 2002.

GardenMama, Tell Me Why, G2C Books, Jackson, MS, 2004.

Getting Started in Southern Gardening, Cool Springs Press, 2005.

Contributor :

Low-Maintenance Gardening, Rodale Press, 1995.

Annuals for Dummies, IDG Press, 1999.

Ortho's All About Greenhouses, Meredith Publishing, 2001.

Ortho's All About Houseplants, Meredith Publishing, 2007.

Your Organic Garden, Your Way

The gardeners I talk to every day are strong on spending time at home, and indeed we invest much of ourselves in the spaces we inhabit. Gardening is a natural part of defining our place in the world. It seems to me that while much of the world seems to spin well out of any individual's sphere of influence, the garden awaits whatever degree of control one exerts. Everyone finds his or her own way. People who swore at the intrusion of lawn mowing into their otherwise sedentary weekend are now gardening and liking it. They tell me they want to know what to do and don't want an education in label reading. They want to spend time in the yard and not be driven crazy by it. Many people who happily tended the grass, shrubs, perennials, and a few annuals for years now want to grow lettuce and fruit because they have concerns about the safety of our food supply.

Younger gardeners get their friends and family involved to create places to relax and entertain at home. They want nice plants to add to the ambiance. Working professionals retreat to the garden on weekends, and retirees, too, find time to garden for its moderate exercise benefits and the sheer amusement it affords. Whether you see yourself in these descriptions, or just want to garden more safely and effectively, I wrote this book for you.

We all are searching for the best methods in gardening. From climate change to personal lifestyles, new factors mean that gardens are different now. Fortunately, the huge shift toward organic gardening methods and philosophy in the twenty-first century is one we can all embrace.

Organic Gardening in the South

Each year, more gardeners ask me about organic gardening, but even though the practices are tried and true here, information tailored to the South can be hard to find. Some people want to address macro concerns like chemical fertilizer runoff's relationship with the Gulf of Mexico's Dead Zone, while others are interested in the potential effects of garden chemicals on their children and their pets. Even those who don't use the term organic gardener ask about its strategies of soil building, non-toxic plant and product choices, composting, mulching, and garden sanitation. This happens because organic methods make sense. They work.

At the same time we are considering what to do and how, the practical, everyday work of growing and maintaining the garden must go on. In the long run, most people just want to garden without a lot of hassle and get straightforward answers when they have questions about their very personal plants. My job daily as a garden communicator on radio, online, and in print is to answer those questions, and to translate horticulture into gardening as I explain what has worked for me and those I admire. I also try to translate sustainable gardening methods into the real world, to make wise gardening ways obvious and doable. I am honored that you have invited me to share my garden attitudes and practices with you.

Gardeners are curious people. Why else would we want to know the name of that flower, try a new tomato, or take a notepad to garden shows? Seeing a plant we chose grow thick and leafy, bloom, and maybe make a berry gives us a sense of accomplishment and puts us in touch with the earth we live on. Keeping a nice yard and garden well maintained gives you those feelings as well, but also adds to your home's bottom line value.

While curiosity alone doesn't make plants thrive, figuring out what will help can be thought provoking. We wonder why blue irises turn white sometimes or a crepe myrtle doesn't bloom despite our best efforts. When there is a problem, usually there is something you can do, but not always, and it's important to know the difference. Gardening is about time, patience, and perspective, or to put it another way, it's like growing up. It doesn't happen all at once: it's all about the long haul, and it's worth it.

Sustainable Gardening: The Issues in Your Hands

For years across the South, the big myth was, "You can't do organic here because we have too many pests and diseases." That is like saying we have no snow, so we shouldn't try to ski! In both cases, we do it our own way. I'm sure your mother disliked the word 'can't' as much as mine did, and persuaded you to try whatever it was. Eggplant casserole and sitting still in a waiting room were my downfall long ago and still are, but I still refuse to say that I can't do either. When you try the strategies in this book, you will no doubt find that some are already in your retinue and others seem likely to work in your situation. I trust the majority will be useful, as they come from gardeners who don't know the word can't. Join us.

Climate change has come. Once upon a time, when I was a girl and Beaver was a television star, it was cold in the winter in northern Louisiana. But the weather has changed and the United States Department of Agriculture has shifted the boundaries of its climate zones accordingly. Smack in the middle of USDA Zone 8 as late as 1990, my home environment is now one hundred miles closer to the Zone 9 line because average temperatures have warmed. That's fine by me in most respects, but the changing zone map (see it at www.arborday.org) may surprise many southern gardeners. To the former Zone 7 folks in southeast Arkansas, Memphis, East Mississippi, much of Alabama, most of Georgia and South Carolina, and eastern North Carolina, I say, "Welcome to Zone 8!" And if you thought you had to go to Jacksonville and Orlando to reach Zone 9, think again. The pattern on Florida's latest map looks like it has been drawn by leaf miners, with parts of the state as far north as the panhandle included in Zone 9. For us gardeners, the differences in average temperatures that we face are compounded by shifts in prevailing winds. We have incredibly wet and painfully dry spells as severe as any of the past century.

The changing conditions mean that we must go beyond the notion of leaving a smaller footprint in this earthly habitat to a stronger idea. I say we must cultivate to grow, both what we have in the our gardens and in the wild places of the South. For example, our region is known for its native and cultivated tree canopy. Over time, though, there are losses due to storms, fires, and human harvests. Our job is to conserve that canopy and its air-cleaning benefits. Unless we continuously plant trees as our forebears have done, both natural forces and our own will eventually leave us naked to the sun. This knowledge should compel us to plant and maintain trees in our gardens and neighborhoods, and to support such conservation projects as Arbor Day observances.

Our habitat's natural beauty and bounty are in our hands and we can adapt our care regimes and visions to sustain and enhance them. Greater awareness of local

microclimate and regional conditions can bring a new vision to our gardens. Trust me on this, the smartest, most practical ways to garden in the 21st century are also the most effective, and with rare exception, they are **classic organic practices updated.** The tasks will be less difficult and the results more rewarding if we keep the big picture in sight: spending time nurturing the garden, not fighting with it. My garden is no Eden, but there's a reason these ways of doing things are called 'practices.' I am strongest on soil improvement and a 'right plant, right place' attitude. Most of all, I try to find and stay in the groove where the flowers, fruit, and vegetables outnumber the weeds and pests.

What Is It About this Region?

Soil conditions and microclimate vary from Memphis to Orlando, but taken altogether, this region is the naturally humid South. Like siblings, we gardeners can spot our differences and argue over them, but in truth we are more like each other than like gardeners in other regions. The differences between us and everybody else affect everything we do in the garden. Factors in plant growth will be discussed elsewhere in the book, but generally speaking, we have hot humid summers, including hot nights that offer little relief to growing plants. Combined with relentless humidity and unpredictable winters, gardening here demands more of plants and gardeners. Further, having three or four growing seasons per year often wears out our soils.

Compared to other regions, things grow differently here. They are lusher (when we say thick hedge, we mean impenetrable) and more tropical. We push the season and our plant selections to grow both vintage plants and hot new selections. We have ideal conditions for a multitude of pests, but also for their predators, if we tend the garden wisely.

Like gardeners in earlier centuries, I learn to grow by word of mouth and by trial and error, both my own and other people's. Experience is an odd thing, as writing this book taught me. For a year, I examined what we actually do in our gardens these days. It's lucky for you that I didn't write it ten or more years ago. Decisions about what to do that seemed complex then have clarity for me now, so it is easier for me to explain my ways and means of growing and keeping plants. Now I see that if you wake up at night worried about the garden, you're doing it wrong.

Gardening isn't always easy, but the harvest is a bonanza in our part of the world. I lived for a time around the corner from a neatly kempt, bountiful vegetable garden and often saw its owner, an older man, as I walked by going to the store. Despite my continued attempts for most of a year, he would not engage in conversation and I never got to ask how he did it all so well, nor compliment him on the elegance of his garden style. No other gardener I've ever met has been so reticent. You've heard them say modestly, "I'm so sorry. You should have been here last week. The garden looked so much better then!" This, while you are walking around open mouthed, trying to take in all the grandeur. Except for this one man, every gardener and horticulturist has been willing to talk plants, commiserate about the weather, and swap seeds and plants. This book adds up all the garden days of my life, the synthesis of my own experience and that of others who have been so generous. Julia Child, the renowned chef, said she never tired of seeing other people's kitchens, because she learned something new in every one. Make that gardens and I agree wholeheartedly.

Growing Things Yesterday and Tomorrow

This book will document gardening in the Deep South (USDA Zones 8 and 9, the way I have learned to do it in fifty or so years of trying. It shocks me to say it, but as I write this, that's how long it's been since I first planted seeds of zinnias and okra as a child.

Everybody who reads gardening books has complaints about them, and I am sure this one will be no different. I have written it to put together what I've learned about growing and maintaining plants. Some of the best teachers have allowed me to soak up the art and science of horticulture and this book allows me to communicate their wisdom in practical terms.

Beyond enough theory and science to explain the task's logic, my explanations will be brief and no doubt seem incomplete to some of my mentors. When I short cut the science, or attempt clumsy analogies, they have my apologies and you have the reference list at the end of the book for clarification and in-depth information on these important topics. In combining what I've gleaned from them with personal and professional experience, I have developed a way of doing things that you can adopt in whole or in part. My hope is that if you have a question about caring for your humid Southern garden, this book will tell you what to do and why and when to do it. If not, it will at least help you define the problems and head you in the right direction.

Gardening is a great hobby, an obsession for some people, but it does take some time for us all. I want you to know what I know, so that the time you spend at it is richly rewarded. This book is organized by strategies that work across plant groups for easy reference. I wrote the book I wanted to own: practical information presented and organized in a way that lets you look it up easily when an issue strikes your fancy or your curiosity.

Gardening is the Key of Life

Life, like gardening, is not a race. Both have a beginning and an end, but it's the middle that counts. The middle is where we mortals take the helm and make things happen. It's what goes on after the seeds are planted and while the sprinklers are running. The part that goes on in between imagining and completing anything is what we live and garden for, and if it is successful, this book will expand the comfort of both.

A garden may not be a song, but it does have a rhythm, a quiet drumbeat that never lets up. A procession of flowers opens one after another as Spring builds to the crescendo of summer. The beat continues in the timpani of rain and Nature's maracas, the cicadas.

The key of a song is its intended best voice, where the composer heard it first and most passionately. Finding the key of your garden may involve changing expectations, picking up a few time-tested tips, and looking for more personal results than perfect plants. To me, the key of my garden's theme song is found in its middle. It's where the improvisation happens, where the riffs and scat singing take off from the sheet music. I know what I'm planting and I have an idea how it's supposed to turn out, but what I do to get there is where I find the key to success in my garden.

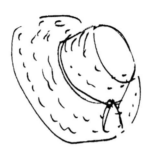

Chapter 1. Soil Strategies for the South

A single garden can contain several soil microclimates. Many plant troubles relate directly to the particular planting place which was chosen. In a container or a garden bed, on a ditch bank, or with lawn all around, the soil in your garden differs in each setting. Few plants tolerate these varied soils and sites equally well. Your job is to match plants with soil, to choose plants suited to the available microclimates, and to expand what's possible by taking reasonable steps to improve growing conditions. Knowing about soil and how it works can help guide your planting decisions.

Many of the soils in the South are humid, a term that describes both their composition and dynamics. These soils use copious amounts of organic matter to maintain good drainage and fertility over time. Think of the plants you like to grow. Each is a native somewhere on the globe, but few reach our gardens directly; more are selected for their adaptability and then propagated for our markets. Plenty are hybrids or even more complicated genetically, bred for the bounteous tomatoes, dense hedges, and large fruits that their parents wouldn't recognize. Because their breeders grew them to perform in corrected, ideal soil, they will not be at their best in unimproved or tired soil.

Even plants native to where you live probably weren't grown in the same soil as their parents enjoyed out in nature. Unless you dug them up yourself, they were grown in a mix made at the propagating nursery. It is clear that depending on the 'as is' soil in your yard to grow the South's popular plants isn't smart even where the native soil is considered good for growing. Displacement of native soils due to construction, layers of topsoil hauled into the site, fill dirt, weather conditions, and even digging and tilling change the soil structure, not always for the better.

Gardening in humid soils is a question of balancing the needs of plants and soils. Our goal is a dynamic system in which the plants use what the soils produce without depleting them. Keeping up with the soil's need for constant replenishment is a challenge made easier by positive actions, just as it is wiser to follow the recipe for a pie you've never made than to try and season it once it's baked. This book aims to be your cookbook for gardening from scratch, to take you from wherever you are to whatever you want to grow.

Components of Soil

Loam rhymes with home, and both are good growing places for most plants and people. Loam has a nearly ideal balance of the clay, silt, and sand that comprise soil, providing a fine place for roots to grow. All soils have some redeeming qualities, but most of the ones we garden in are decidedly not ideal. Alas, they are not loam.

Clay. Everyone knows that cups, plates, and flower pots can be made from clay, which has a dense, mineral-rich consistency. Soils that are primarily clay feel sticky to touch. Clay soil is heavy and does not leak, which is good up to a point, but can challenge the gardener. Once clay soil is water-logged or turned to powder by dry conditions, it is very difficult to dry out or rewet and so it is stressful to plants.

Sand. You can feel sand between your toes, and sandy soils have delightful, natural grit. In reasonable amounts, sand cuts through clay and is a benefit, but alone, it is challenging for almost all gardeners to cultivate. Particles of sand are much larger than those of clay and different from it chemically.

Silt. Sized between tiny clay and relatively large sand particles in soil, and also between them chemically, there is silt. Unlike sand or clay, pure silt feels like flour or talcum powder to the touch.

The soil spectrum. The visible components of all soils can be divided into a soil spectrum by their relative size. There are some plants that can grow in any position on the spectrum, but a garden by definition is a cultivated space. We grow many different kinds of plants, native, naturalized, and exotic in origin and some are better suited than others to the stresses our of region. Building soil structure and conditions that can host the garden plants you want to grow is the surest path to success in the humid south.

Though small, some of the the components of the soil spectrum can be seen. Roughly, here are relative sizes, left to right, of minerals; clay; peat and alternatives; compost; perlite; and ground bark. Other grindings like gin moat and stable shavings may be larger, while there are many microscopic organic and inorganic substances in the mix, also.

Test your Drainage

When in doubt about how well your soil drains, test it by digging a hole 12 inches wide and a bit deeper. Fill it with water and hope for a steady, even percolation into the soil. If you have trouble filling the hole because it drains so quickly, or if the water doesn't drain completely in 30 minutes, the range of plants that will grow well is limited. The solution to both drainage problems is the addition of organic matter to the native soil.

Good soil does the job. Even sandy soils have a percentage of submicroscopic clay in them; it is the clay that binds with water and absorbs nutrients into the pipes, the vascular system of the plant. When water flows through sandy soil too quickly, the clay stays dry and the plant suffers. Conversely, when water sits in the root zone for too long, the clay swells up, crushing the roots, and the plant suffers.

The gardener's goal for soil is good tilth. This quality is hard to define, but relatively easy to see and feel. Soil with good tilth can be worked without destroying its structure. When you crush a clod that is no more than moderately wet or dry, it neither turns to powder nor sticks to itself, a tool, or your hand. In the nursery pot and in the garden, there is good soil and bad soil, at least from the gardener's perspective. Good garden soil and good potting mix drain well enough for the plants growing in it, smell earthy-nice, and keep their brown color without crusting. You wouldn't build a house without a foundation, and you should give your plants that solid underpinning, too, by amending the soil.

The Living Earth Beneath Our Feet

Deciding what to grow and how to do it starts by looking down. It's all about the soil we have today and the soil we can have if we take care of the earth beneath our feet. The soil in your garden is the key to garden success, both this season and in the long term.

On a hot summer day, it is easy to see the difference between healthy garden soil and its alternative. Rich brown, crumbly soil with a slight edgy grit will need only moderate amounts of water even in drought, yet remain unsaturated in all but the worst monsoon season. Gray or red clay, gumbo, or sandy soils will not.

Enhancing the Subterranean Habitat

When you learn about life underground and how to nurture it, you understand that enhancing the subterranean habitat is just as important as working with the garden we can see. I did indeed come to love the worms, roliepolies, lizards and even some of the spiders in the gardens of my childhood. I learned that the mushrooms in the yard grew where the mimosa tree used to be, and not to eat them or the pokeberries in the woods—the former were poisonous and the latter more important as warpaint. These fascinating discoveries were, however, secondary to the dirt itself in my estimation, even then. We actually made mudpies in those days, and I was the champ.

The soil food web. As much time as I spent with my hands and knees in the dirt, I couldn't have known the panorama of life I was carrying around on my muddy jeans. Even after studying horticulture in college, I couldn't have known, since it took electron microscopy to reveal the natural, truly amazing ingenuity of the soil food web. It is ironic that something we have always known can finally be understood empirically, not just taken on faith. Soil has the ability to sustain itself: after

drum type composter

all, no one fertilizes the swamp and yet it teems with plant life. Better yet, the same natural principles can transform home garden soil and make your job as gardener more rewarding from day one. The good things you do for your soil ensure its future health.

Dig the Truth

Here's a secret: when the soil works well, it's easier to grow plants. They look better, bear more, and are less vulnerable to pests. Organic practices are the way to achieve this blissful state of growth. You're probably making some of these smart garden moves:

Composting leaves, kitchen waste, and garden debris instead of bagging them for trash. Using nutritious homemade compost saves you time and money on purchases and transport of soil amendments and fertilizer. Each time you complain about increasing taxes, and then add to the size of the landfill with compostables, think about it.

Choosing the right plant for the place. Optimal variety selection is a hallmark of wise gardeners. It's not to limit your plant choices, but to give you a place to start. There are hundreds of plants at the smallest, niche nursery on any given day, and it's a boon to know which one grew for someone else in a setting similar to your own. If one tomato is more likely to beat the blight than others, let me know about it!

Walking the garden daily to exercise body and mind. You won't miss the first flowers, or the toad that's taken up residence, or the last zinnias before frost. Seeing problems develop lets you deal with the first pests, not the third generation of a geometrically expanding population.

Keeping tidy. Sanitation simply means cleaning up plant debris and keeping the weeds down to reduce the places pests can hide and wait to ambush your plants. Most debris can be composted, but trash any particularly noxious weeds unless you can be certain the compost pile will heat up above 120 degrees.

Reducing toxic waste. Reducing the use of pesticides, whether organic in origin or not, on your property and encouraging these approaches where you live greatly decreases the amount of potentially toxic waste generated and the cost for municipal disposal.

Recycling. Recycle not only leaves but also the plastics when possible. My grandmother preached this adage: Use it up, wear it out, make it do, or do without. Since she cut wax milk cartons to make rooting pots and used egg cartons to sprout seeds, I'm sure she'd like these five ways to reuse a plastic gallon jug.

*Use
Recycled
Gallon
Jugs For
Many Jobs*

*make a hot cap
with ventilator top*

*punch holes for a drip
watering reservoir*

*use for mixing
fertilizer*

1. Cut the bottom out of a gallon jug but leave the top and cap in place. Use this as a a hotcap or cover for tender seedlings on cool nights. Remember to remove the bottlecap or the whole top each morning for ventilation, depending on the weather.

2. Make a reservoir: use an icepick or small screwdriver to make holes in the sides close to the bottom of the jug. Bury it next to melons or pumpkins and keep it full of water with a bit of fertilizer for these insatiable vines.

3. The jugs make an easy mixing container for fertilizer. The measure is standard, has a removable top and is lighter than traditional watering cans. Or if your can isn't marked, use the jug to mix the correct amount and pour it into the watering can.

4. Slice off the top at a wide angle, leaving the handle. Use it to scoop potting soil and amendments. Or use it for dipping up water from a rain barrel or stream and distributing it.

5. In times of vacation or serious drought, use the reservoir idea for tomatoes and young trees.

Amending Your Soil

Facing down a patch of native soil for the first time can be a daunting experience if you're not prepared. The good news is this: when you amend the humid soils of the South, they work better, longer. When you do the basics of soil prep on the front end, before you plant, maintenance is much easier later on. Perhaps best of all, soils that weren't amended before the plants were installed can be helped, too. This is especially heartening to homebuyers who discover too late

that the garden they hoped to tend doesn't respond to their efforts. Upon digging around under the mulch, they find compacted soil or no actual soil at all, just whatever fill was brought in to level the site. This chapter includes approaches I use to improve soil structure in both situations.

Tools

The work starts here. If you don't know these basic tools, say hello and get acquainted. If you do, keep the blades clean and sharp. In a perfect garden, there would be a bucket of sand to plunge the shovel and trowel in to keep them clean and dry between uses. There are tools for every task. If a task takes forever or hurts your back, perhaps you are not using the proper tool. Here are the main tools that most gardeners will need.

Cultivators are clever tools for loosening soil and grabbing weeds. Most have three clawlike tines on a short handle, but long handled versions let you work from farther away, either standing up or sitting on a low stool. Reducing the number of tasks that make you hunch over is smart, no matter your age.

Shovels of several sorts. **Traditional shovels and spades** are unbeatable if they are the right size for you. They should fit your grip and lift levels. Try before you buy if at all possible, but not by digging a hole at the garden center. Pick up the tool, hoist it over your shoulder, and assume the digging position. Be sure your foot fits the shelf at the top of the blade and that the handle is smooth and solidly attached. Smaller, **mini-shovels** have handles about three feet long and are really more like big trowels or small scoops. They're handy for spreading compost and turning potting soil.

A **sharpshooter** is a shovel with a long, narrow blade usually with a T-shaped grip on a four-foot handle. The name may be odd, but the tool does get you closer to the target when digging up small trees and dividing perennials. The T grip spreads the energy you're expending, increasing the digging power of the sharpshooter and other tools fitted with this kind of handle.

Forks and scoops. Forks are made for digging or pitching hay, depending on the thickness and curve of the tines. Straight, wide-tined digging forks turn heavy soil and amendments well, but a slightly curved pitchfork with narrower tines will be easier on you when turning compost or moving pinestraw.

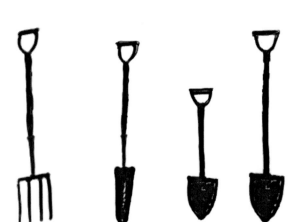

Tools, left to right:
compost fork
sharpshooter
short-handled spade
long-handled spade

A lightweight, oversized **manure or snow scoop** is a great tool to have if you need to move large piles of compost, sand, or almost anything else that would take all day with a classic shovel.

Tillers can be rented readily, and unless you are embarking on an estate-size garden, it's the way to go. Once beds for lawns, ornamentals, or edibles are made, a tiller becomes something your friends borrow and you maintain. You'll likely rent more horsepower than you would buy for an affordable price. Maintenance and storage stay off your list, and you can call for help if a rented tool gives you trouble. In fact, tilling the same area every year can be counterproductive to good soil health. The concepts of low-till and no-till approaches to farming are well-documented. I have tilled my vegetable beds twice in the last decade, but other than that they are easily dug by hand. The oldest bed in my garden was tilled once in the last century and might get completely renovated by 2010.

Compost is Good. Make Some.

Starting a compost pile couldn't be easier. Rake up fallen leaves into a pile about three feet cubed behind the shrubs and let it be. Come back in spring and turn it over to see the great state of decomposition. It is ready to dig into a new bed or become a half-inch deep blanket around shrubs, trees, and perennials.

Options are plentiful for those who prefer a more formal approach than my informal piles or 'time is on my side' attitude toward composting. Especially where spaces are small, simply containing the pile keeps it neat and lowers its visibility. Put short fencing on three sides with a 'gate or removable side on the fourth for access. Any material, from welded wire to wooden pickets to recycled pallets, will do so long as it has slats or other ventilation. To speed the compost process along, open the gate once a week and turn the pile. A second bin to turn into makes the whole thing even easier. A third bin allows you to both turn the pile and stagger its completion times by starting new ones at intervals.

Bin composters are popular with gardeners with less volume to compost than a good pile requires. Aeration is accomplished with holes in the drum, and a crank hand handle takes care of turning it while giving your arms a brief workout.

Vermicomposters have their own benefits. Earthworm castings are a nutritional

boon to flower beds, they'll gleefully recycle old newspaper, and everything necessary takes up less space than a dorm refrigerator.

If you plan to blanket a lawn or add compost to a seedbed, you will want to screen or sift it. Use 1/4 -1/2 inch mesh, or window screen for material to add like peat to potting mix.

Blankets of compost differ from mulch in that you can work the compost into the top few inches of the soil. Mulch should be stable enough to last at least one season before it rots enough to work in or remove to the compost pile.

Bags of compost alone or mixed with manure are readily available. The contents of a bag of topsoil are questionable at best, while compost and manure sources or types are usually listed on their bags. Humus is another iffy material until you have tried a particular brand. All are some sort of organic matter and if their composition and cost suit you, use them as one arrow in your quiver of OMs (organic materials).

To take basic rotted leaf compost to the next level, real compost, add grass clippings and kitchen waste like celery and lettuce trimmings. Try to keep the ratio two parts brown to one part green. Turning the pile aerates it, and the more often you do it, the faster it rots. Collect kitchen scraps in a covered container (far right).

Raised Beds

Rethink your notion of a raised bed. My mother built brick raised beds because we lived by the river and the yard stayed very wet at times in that area. Yours don't have to be that high, or that solid, unless you want to fit them with hinged glass tops to create cold frames or hot beds. In fact, most every garden bed in these parts is at least slightly raised. Even in well-drained soil, beds made a couple of inches above ground level work better.

How to Dig a New Bed, Step by Step

Mark the space for the bed with string, plumbers chalk or spray paint.

Scrape off anything growing there now using a square spade's sharp edge. Try to get the plants and as little soil as possible with each pass. Conventional gardening advice would say to simply turn existing green matter over into the soil. In our region that practice can be a roadmap to Weedville since so many of our worst weeds like bermuda grass and dollar weed will survive to sprout another day. Compost such troublemakers with caution, too.

Dig a standard shovel's depth into the soil, turning each shovelful over to expose its innards to the sun. Or till to the same depth: four to six inches on average is fine. Do not overwork the soil or dig much deeper.

If time permits, leave the soil turned over for a few days and pull out any remaining weeds or roots. Should heavy rain threaten, skip this step.

Turn the shovel blade away from you and chop large chunks into smaller ones.

Begin adding amendments in order of their size, largest first. Start with ground bark and leaf mold, then manure and compost (a total of four to six inches maximum), finally no more than an inch of sand, a sprinkling of garden lime, and complete fertilizer or individual elemental organic fertilizers in granular forms.

Feed the soil first, then feed the plants. This approach ensures that plant roots have access to and can use what's available.

Till or turn after each addition, or if using a truckload of prepared planting mix, do so after each two inches is laid on top, then dig in another two inches if needed for good tilth.

Think of the whole business as gumbo; if everything is not well mixed, the overall taste is affected. You can still see each component, and don't want it pureed. This is most likely the only time you'll do this much work on this particular bed, so grin and go ahead.

Rake the bed into a loaf shape, with a gentle slope down to ground level all the way around. Mulch the bed.

Use a shovel to cut a neat 'V'-shaped edge between the bed and the lawn, or install a frame or edging as you wish.

Time permitting, let the bed rest for some length of time before planting. A week is okay, a month is better, half a year is fine, too.

Soil dynamics. Know that the elements will begin the ancient dance of the micros and macros, and the new bed will settle, in some areas very quickly as clay soil reveals its many sides and organic matter gets to rotting. This dynamic soil habitat will ultimately be about two inches above ground level and four well-cultivated inches below and building.

Keep established beds in condition with compost blankets in spring, worked in and topped by mulch. In fall, work in the rotting mulch and replace it. If you use shredded or straw mulches, rake them out after a year or two and replace completely. Their strong fibers can mat once true decomposition gets going.

Container Concerns

Gardeners take to containers for practical and aesthetic reasons. Face it, after reading about the joys of amending soil, mixing soil for potted plants sounds easy, and it is, when you follow the recipes below.

Even if you have garden beds, a row of ferns hanging from the front porch rafters seems more than a decorative touch. It's the way to grow for drama and southern style. You gain control over water, fertilizer, even sunlight and daylength conditions when you grow potted plants. Whether you go for seasonal annuals on the deck or collect orchids, the variety of plants you can grow is unsurpassed, indoors and out.

But we've always done that! Trendy as container gardening has become lately, southerners have always had a pot of hen and chicks or mother-in-law's tongue around someplace. Nowadays fancy and stupendous pots are available and affordable, but we keep a stack of black plastic growing pots around, too, for propagating and holding over. We keep daylilies and iris divisions dug after flowering and summer garden center bargains in pots until fall to avoid transplant shock. Then we might reuse those same pots again to start perennial seeds for planting the next spring.

Used to be, pots were plastic or terra cotta clay. If you considered yourself a serious gardener and had the money, you bought clay and treasured it. Terra cotta must be soaked before planting, then scrubbed clean before reusing because either algae or fertilizer residue spoils its good looks and growing qualities. It also needs watering more often than a plastic pot of comparable size, freezes faster, and eventually shatters. Still, the classic look and excellent root zone conditions terra cotta offers for many plants keep it on every shelf. Right there with it are the new plastic pots and other materials we've come to love. Durable, colorful, and produced with multiple drainage holes, lightweight plastics are readily sculpted into every size and shape a designer can imagine. Many designs with hollow, rounded rims mimic the look of terracotta, without the weight. Pottery, glazed ceramic, concrete, and resins have gained attention, and cocoa fiber sheets have taken over from sphagnum moss for basket liners.

Rules and Guidelines

To be used as a growing container, a thing must be able to **hold enough soil** and roots to support the plant, and must have drainage. Everything else about the way it looks and what it is made of is either a design consideration or driven by the economics of its manufacture.

Nothing is more important to growing plants in pots than this: **water must pass through the soil and out the drainage hole(s) regularly,** preferably each time you water. In fact, to water correctly, water until you fill the headspace above the soil and below the rim of the pot. Let that percolate through the soil and refill the headspace again. If you are growing cacti, the next watering may not be necessary for weeks. Tomatoes will require almost daily irrigation even with this method.

If the soil doesn't get leached (the horticultural term for the process described above), roots die. Place pots or elevate them as needed to be sure drainage isn't blocked. If you use saucers or trays under pots, never allow water that has passed through the soil to stand. Dump it out or suck it up with a siphon or turkey baster. When leach water is reabsorbed through the roots, it is toxic and causes problems such as tip burn, especially among members of the huge Lily family such as amaryllis and dracaena.

Potting mixes that sustain most plants successfully are well-drained, organic, and create root zones that allow plenty of feeder roots to move water and nutrients into the plant's vascular system to the stems, leaves, and flowers. Pre-packaged potting mixes vary widely, and so do their results. If the contents of a bag are heavy, wet, or smelly, dump it in the compost pile where it can do some good. At the other end of the spectrum are ultra lightweight mixes full of perlite and finely shredded peat. Reserve those for starting seeds or rooting African violet leaves.

Most potting soil you buy in a bag has an organic base, a drainage element, and fertilizer. Many also have water-holding gels designed to reduce the need to water as often. I do not use them, but if you do, add a bit less compost or compost/manure or a bit more sand to offset their water-holding actions. Quality products are not cheap and contain good elements, but nothing on the market is as good as the mixes you can tailor to your plants and gardening habits. Excellent, pine bark-based potting soils are made in our part of the world from homegrown resources and are becoming more available across the region every year.

21

GardenMama's Recipe
Better Potting Soil Than You Can Buy:

1 big bag pine bark-based or other quality potting soil. Dump the contents into a wheelbarrow to mix and save the bag for measuring:

½ bag ground pine or hardwood bark. Be sure its ground, not shredded or nuggets.

½ bag compost or compost/manure. I do not use manure in soils that will grow edibles of any sort.

¼ bag sharp sand or sandbox sand.

1 cup granular garden fertilizer (5-10-10). This product can be made for vegetable or flower gardens. Look for an organic formula.

1 cup garden lime (not hydrated)

Mix very well. I use a short shovel with a square blade five inches wide.

Store indefinitely in a plastic tub or garbage can.

Soil sifter

Potting Soil Variations

Tailor the basic potting soil recipe to suit the plant groups you are growing.

-Add ¼ bag manure and 1 cup cottonseed or other organic nitrogen to make a mix for roses and shrubs. To avoid possible contamination, substitute additional compost for the manure if growing vegetables, herbs, or anything edible.

Add more:

-compost for cuttings, houseplants, and small pots of annuals.

-sharp sand for succulents, Mediterranean and New Zealand annuals like Bacopas. Perennial Dianthus and many kinds of herbs like this too.

-ground bark in larger pots for better drainage.

-lime and fertilizer when adding larger quantities of bark.

Mix soil and bark for equally for orchids, poinsettias, and other plants that need really great drainage.

<u>Chapter Two. Plants and How to Work with Them</u>

It would be hard to trim your toenails if you didn't know them from your elbow. When you know what the various plant parts are and what they do for a living, you can understand the factors that bring on thrifty growth and how to encourage what you want when you want it. (You remember, of course, that part of the joy of gardening is the ability to control your corner of the world at least sometimes.) At transplanting time, it's good to know how roots work as you consider how to favor their new start. Likewise, when abundant flowers elude you, it's smart to examine what will get them going based on knowledge of which plant parts work together to bring forth the blooms.

Finally, knowing a bit of botany helps along the way to the DisneyWorld of garden amusements, propagation. Watching seeds poke their noses up from the soil is awesome; being the one to coax live roots from a bare stem is intoxicating. Some plant groups will send roots out all along any cut stem, some only sprout at the nodes. **Learning about plant parts and the ways they arrange themselves can be thought of as learning the language of gardening.** Becoming fluent in 'gardenspeak' informs your growing strategies, as well as your ability to diagnose and treat problems that arise. Understanding this information tells you what the various parts do, so you can help them do it.

Botany Briefly: Plant Parts

Roots can be compared to the Push Me Pull You in the tales of Dr. Doolittle. Roots push into soil, but the tiny root hairs that cover them actually pull. The **root hairs** absorb nutrient-rich water from the spaces between soil particles and develop symbiotic relationships with the microorganisms in the soil solution. All this happens so the roots can pump water and food up to the aboveground plant parts. Together the roots and root hairs are the anchors that hold the plant in its place and are its main lifeline. Without roots, water and nutrients must be provided to the plant via the air as some are, but healthy roots are imperative to most plants.

Stems, branches, and trunks move water and nutrients through the plant. Think of them as straws that operate ideally when appropriate pressures are applied in the presence of adequate supplies. When you, or a tree canopy, suck on a straw, plenty of good can happen if the glass, or soil moisture reservoir, is full.

Stems, like eyelashes, can be thick or thin, but are always essential. Lashes act as filters, and so do stems in this way: at one end of a stem is a supporting branch and at the other is a leaf or a flower, or both. The water and nutrients that travel through the stem supply the juice that directs the plant to expand its cells and develop the next leaf or

Photosynthesis is the process that turns the water and nutrients into energy to grow the plant in the presence of light.

flower. The internal chemistry of each plant determines what and when all that happens, and the stem is the plant part that delivers that message and sees it is received. Not all plants have branches and trunks, but most of them have stems.

Branches work like arms to reach into the world above the base of the plant. As one kind of tubing, they supply vital water and nutrients to the canopy of whatever grows above ground. But their effect goes beyond the internal plumbing to outer beauty and stunning levels of support for leaves, flowers, and fruits. Considering how much a tree's worth of plums or pears can weigh, it's a bit of a miracle that more branches don't break under the load. It is the remarkable ability of many branches to know when to quit. They self-prune, dropping leaves and even sacrificing some of their own as they dry up parts to survive stressful times. We've all seen perennial clumps shut down from the top to their base; their stems and branches control those seasonal changes. Besides, birds' nests, squirrel racetracks, and leafy shade wouldn't have much chance without the branches of shrubs and trees.

Trunks are exquisitely adapted to their tasks, supporting growth and moderating the impact of climate on trees. Rugged or smooth, their bark is an overcoat, protecting the tender pipes inside.

Adapted Plant Parts

Both roots and stems have the ability to adapt their growth to store water and nutrients. **Rhizomes,** often mistakenly thought of as roots, are adapted, horizontal stems that can be almost woody. Iris is the most common example of rhizomes. Now that you know what the purpose of the rhizome is to store energy to grow the plant and now that you know it is a long, sort of sideways structure, their planting needs make sense. Rhizomes need to be nestled into

rhizome

the soil longways, with an exposed side. Since new shoots will grow from the top and roots from the bottom, one needs soil and the other needs light to thrive.

Tubers and tuberous roots. Tubers are a bit different from the other groups. If you've ever seen potato still attached to its stem, you know it is a repository of carbohydrate and sugars. The identifying characteristic here is the eye. Potatoes and caladiums are tubers and must have eyes to sprout and grow. Some plants have swollen tubers which are adapted roots instead of adapted stems. The exact part that swells up doesn't make much difference, except that the underground parts of tuberous begonias, sweet potatoes, dahlias, cannas and daylilies look different from the others. Daylilies, with obviously swollen roots, are perhaps the easiest to distinguish.

potato tuber

left, daffodil bulb; right, lily bulb

Bulbs like daffodil and hyacinth have classic parts that define the group: little roots, or root initials (that means they haven't quite taken off yet), that are attached to a flat bottom called a basal plate. The rest of the thing is called its scales, which are just the morphed form of the leaves that wrap around next year's flower bud.

Corms are like a simpler form of bulbs. Gladiolas, freesias, and crocuses are three corms that lots of people grow, but gloxinia also grows from a corm, as does that bane of so many gardens, common crocosmia. They lack the scales of the true bulbs, but have the roots and basal plate, and are simply swollen stems.

corms

The remaining plant parts seem to get all the press: **flowers, fruit, and seeds.** Flowers can be male, female, or both, productive or sterile, but their job is always to advertise. They grab the eye and feet of those essential garden denizens, the pollinators, and grace your table or lapel with equal aplomb. In reality, though, the reason for all that wild coloration and those exotic shapes is to get the precious pollen from anther to stigma. Flowers offer nectar to the birds and insects in exchange for moving the goods. They'll sing, dance, and light up like a neon sign in a roadhouse window to get the travelers to stop by. Honeybees are searching for pollen as well as nectar, but most are simply seeking nectar and distribute pollen in the process.

Pollinators carry or shake pollen on to the next flower along their way. The fruits of their labors really bridge the span from hope to reality, in that they succor the flower on its journey to ensuring the future of that plant and its species. Quality pollination is crucial to fruit set and viable seed development.

Protective of the seed itself, fruit is often attractive to the mammals that distribute it as they move around or eat it. Their anatomy then facilitates its dispersal to a distant location, to put it delicately.

Seeds are the plant's estate, its legacy to future generations. Its DNA holds the key to the way a flower is shaped, the aroma it uses to attract pollinators or repel predators, and the way the fruit will taste. The variety in seeds is incredible, but the methods they use to increase their odds of survival are spiritual in their brilliance. When pollination occurs in the natural course of events in the garden, natural mixing of seed lines often occurs. We grow corn of one variety in a square pattern (four by four feet at least) to ensure that the pollen from one corn plant will be blown, jostled or carried to its neighbors of the same species, not wafted over the beans or peas. Here we aren't trying to breed a new corn, we are just making sure the ears will fill with kernels because they are well-pollinated from among their own kind. When we grow two different kinds of plums or persimmons next to each other, we're hoping for cross pollination. Though both

The pollinators: who are these guys?

The pollinators in our gardens are some species of honeybees and bumblebees, wasps, syrphid flies, certain butterflies and moths, some ants, thrips, and a few people, not necessarily in that order. Bats, hummingbirds, and lizards pollinate, and so do possums and rodents occasionally. It seems like there are plenty of all these creatures around, so why waste time worrying about pollination? Pollination is essential for plant reproduction and fruit. What you do in your own backyard makes a difference in pollinator populations, which goes directly to the number and quality of any produce you might grow. By providing pollinators a place to rest safe from predators, to nest and breed, along with food and water resources, your impact multiplies.

will make some fruit alone, if everything else is working well for the trees, two varieties together make for a larger and tastier harvest.

You can't save all seed, but you should save some for the sake of the future of cultivated plants. When we grow only one type of zinnia or one petunia or one wheat, we limit not only our vase and table. Monocropping means if one plant sneezes, the entire planting catches cold. By cultivating more than one kind, we help to ensure the survival of all the variations of that plant. Its DNA holds the keys to the unknown attributes it carries. Cold hardiness, pest repulsion, growth habit, and untold uses in medicine are borne in those seeds. If lima beans in one area are unable to bear because climate change, a plant breeder can theoretically cross it with a relative to gain heat tolerance, providing the other variety still exists. Seed-bearing plants may be open-pollinated, stable hybrids like cherry tomatoes and certain other heirloom varieties. Or they may be recently bred hybrids which deliver good garden results straight from the seed packet, but if allowed to intermingle and go to seed, will deliver an unpredictable next generation. Unless you are particularly curious about what might come from them, or want to make crosses yourself, hybrid seeds are not for saving.

Storing seed, whether mine, yours, or someone else's, is a complex topic. There are volumes written on the best way to harvest, clean, and store seed. For my limited efforts, cleaning seed is easy enough if you have a piece of window screen and a box. Break open the dry pods if needed and screen what's inside to segregate the seeds. In all but very extreme circumstances, usually dictated by the person giving me the seed, I store seed of all sorts in paper envelopes, labeled with date and name. The envelopes or seed packs go into two big canisters, one for flowers and one for vegetables, recycled from gifts of holiday popcorn. The cans sit in my office where temperatures are pleasant and humidity low.

Refrigeration might extend some seeds lives, and other gardeners swear by freezing their seeds. I don't find those measures necessary, but I do make it a point not to get seeds wet nor bake them by leaving seed packs outdoors. Seed are the future, but any joy that we take in viewing or eating these plant parts is entirely secondary to their reason for being.

Family Ties: Major Plant Groups And How They Grow

Here are the major plant groups with my growing notes. Please understand that my classifications are gardenesque, not necessarily horticultural. The first groups are green-stemmed, or herbaceous plants.

Annuals

Some gardeners in other climates consider us fortunate to have at least two and sometimes three seasons to plant annuals each year. It is true that annuals alone can bring color, texture, wildly patterned leaves, outrageous flowers, and in some cases, food, to containers and garden beds. Annual plants, whether flowers, herbs, grasses, or vegetables, exist to produce a seed during one season and die soon afterwards. That's their nature, and it explains why annuals are heavy feeders and why water stress can be their downfall.

Deadheading. Growing annuals successfully means removing flowers as they fade. Once the flowers are allowed to mature into seedheads, that annual's season is over. You deadhead to prevent the process from proceeding naturally until and if you want them to set seed.

Self-cleaning wax begonias drop their flowers naturally, but most annuals will set far more new buds if you deadhead them. If you cut flowers regularly for vases, you probably cut stems as long as possible. Otherwise, cut the fading flower off its stem just above the first true leaf below the bloom.

Pinching back. Besides deadheading, many annuals respond well to pinching as a means of coaxing new branches to create more tips that bear flower buds. To pinch, reach below the flower to the second or even the third set of leaves under it and pinch or snip the stem at that point. New branches will emerge from that point and sometimes others below, often on both sides of the stem. This process is particularly effective when growing members of the Mint family, such as coleus, distinguished by square stems.

Growing conditions. Make friends with fertilizer and its companion, water, to grow and maintain the finest annual beds or pots in town. Almost universally, annuals thrive in rich, well-drained soil. The exceptions don't need conditions as rich but can usually tolerate them. Start with small plants (four inch pots or smaller) early in the season, water often enough so the soil drains but doesn't dry out (maybe daily at first when planting in the summer, more like twice a week for impatiens in March). Nearly constantly available fertilizer makes all the difference for the first weeks after planting. Supply it in a soluble form, as often as the label of your particular product allows, or use it slightly more often at half-strength. Be relentless about the water and fertilizer program until the plants are blooming. At that point you can decide whether to back off a bit or continue. If the plants are large enough to suit you, its time to move to a maintenance routine. Don't let the plants wilt or become pale. Do water at least weekly and fertilize at least monthly

Perennials

A **perennial** is a plant with fleshy, non-woody stems that is not an annual. It has a crown, a dense mass in the middle which is essential to its existence. Indeed, perennials live to nurture this heart so that after the plant blooms and sets seed this season, the crown can survive to grow again next year. It is your job to respect the crown: mulch up to, but not over it, and cut flower stems down to but not into it. As soon as perennials go dormant, not months later, be there with the snips to cut the brown stems down and rake out the clump. Such good garden sanitation and decent air circulation around perennial plants prevents many pests from getting a foothold in the environment.

These plants grow by expanding the size of the crown itself and by sprouting new plants. These baby plants are clones of the first, often sprouted from runners and located around or to one side of the mother plant. Other perennials, including ones that would like to send runners but are hopelessly crowded, sprout new plants at their base. If the lower part of some perennial stems rest on the ground, new plants will sprout at the nodes (growing points) along the stem.

Dividing perennials. Divide perennials on demand, less by the calendar and more by observing the plants. The green thumber's rule is to dig up perennials and separate the clump into pieces, then replant or pot up. Look at the plants when they bloom to note if they are as floriferous as last year, or if new plants are crowding each other badly. Whatever species it is, that's the time to dig and divide the perennial. Another green thumber rule is to dig and divide perennials in the season opposite their bloom. But that doesn't always work. Here's why:

But not always...

Strawberry is an example of a plant widely grown as an annual despite its botanical designation as a perennial. By planting strawberries in fall for spring harvest, we escape the inevitable insects and diseases of summer which often devastate the plants.

Hollyhock is actually a biennial, a plant that grows for one season and blooms for the first time the next. But in much of the south, spring's small plants often bloom before frost that same year, then overwinter.

Early spring blooming perennials that are very crowded may choke by fall if you wait until then to divide. Wait a month after early phlox and daisies bloom, then dig, divide, and replant them while there is an entire growing season for them to get established. Clumps that grow crowded during the current season can be worked in the fall, weather permitting.

Fall flowering perennials would logically be worked in the spring, but some years it seems that one day it's New Years and the next the hostas have sprouted and it is still too wet to work the soil. Let the first frost knock down the stems, then get to work on the clumps while soil conditions are good, instead of waiting out the weather next spring.

Summer brings on a host of perennial flowers such as black-eyed Susan, yarrow, lantana, and coneflower, and by the rule, you'd divide them in winter. Some might admit they've done this occasionally, when the winter is especially mild and gardeners get cabin fever. It is not a great idea, though, since winter is nothing if not changeable in these parts. Instead, cut them down as they go dormant, but wait to dig and divide until early spring, weather permitting.

My style and the weather. The caveat, 'weather permitting,' plays a huge role in my style of gardening, and I suggest you cultivate this attitude, too, when planting and digging plants of all sorts. Forcing tasks only because someone said or wrote that it is Time to Do Something in the garden is folly. Perennials are more forgiving than some of the other plant groups when it comes to moving them around the garden, but drought stricken or boggy soil is no help to their roots. Likewise, fertilizing perennials is often a matter of timing. Ideally, you'll plant them in soil rich in compost with a granular flowering formula fertilizer worked in. Probably, you'll find space in a bed already made and use a soluble fertilizer to water the new perennial into its space. Speaking of space, ample space between plants is essential to good air circulation around them. Crowded perennials are stressed: they do not bloom properly, may die out in the middle, and will be more vulnerable to pests and diseases. Part of the balancing act with

PERENNIAL INSURANCE

Always buy two or three of a new plant or one big enough to take a cutting from immediately. Plant separately or leave one in a pot if you're unsure where they'll thrive.

No matter what else you do or don't do, clean up the perennial garden in the winter. Cut back all of the dormant plant material and rake out the old leaves and flowers left in the bed. Work in the mulch if it has begun to decompose, and replenish it.

29

perennials is to feed them enough to get flowers and thrifty growth, but not too much. Too much in this case means all leaves and no flowers, or weak stems that flop over. Too little sun for the particular species will also cause these problems.

My fertilizer regime for perennials is quite simple, weather and my watering habits permitting. Here are my guidelines:

> When new growth starts in spring, or when planting new clumps any time, spread a half inch blanket of compost around the base of the plant. (I make my own, and hope you will, too, but you can buy good bagged products or a truckful at the garden center. If you purchase compost with manure in it, use a bit less.) Work that material into the top inch or so of garden bed.

> Wait to fertilize again until the new growth is several inches tall. This might be anytime during the year, depending on species. For example, I fertilize native phlox in early spring before daylilies and iris because they start to grow sooner in my garden. But Lenten rose really takes off in fall, so I fertilize it around Thanksgiving. Start using a flower formula fertilizer, either granular or water-soluble. The products are covered in the fertilizer section, but use your choice as often as the label allows for three applications or until the plants begin blooming, whichever happens first. Then, if you want the plants to grow at their maximum, keep it up.

> If the growing season is rainy, fertilizers that can be sprayed onto plant leaves can be very effective. In very dry times, remember to water the plants before fertilizing with any material.

Perennializing. To offset the heartbreak of discovering there are some delightful plants that fail to embrace our hot, humid world and turn to mush, some plants stick around longer than expected. Embrace the rogues that perennialize, such as annual 'Telstar' dianthus in Zone 8 and tropical airplane plants in lower Zone 8 and 9. Sometimes a clump simply doesn't die, other times it's a neat reseeder that replenishes itself, such as Mexican hat.

Bulbs and Plants That Act Like Them

Bulbs are loosely defined here as anything swelled up that you plant, including true bulbs, corms, tubers, rhizomes, and tuberous roots. It's an amazing thing to realize that bulbs have evolved to be so self sufficient, and it's probably the result of their native environment's challenges. Extreme climate conditions may cause plants to hunker down, genetically speaking. Prolonged drought or frigid temperatures winnow out those that can't adapt to survive. The strong survive to the next year, as leaves transfer their nutrients into the roots, and sit there, waiting for conditions to improve. True bulbs, certainly, and many of the others

are the jack-in-the-box of plant materials: excitement is there, just squashed down, ready to spring when released.

Fertilizer. I grow bulbs mostly as perennials, like spider lily, iris, canna, and daffodils, knowing they'll be in the ground for several years at least. Their soil must be a place where the bulblike structures they use for storing energy can rest and gain strength for the following year. They are not demanding, usually not needing any more than moderate amounts of water and with a few notable exceptions, are not prone to pests. Fertilize perennial bulbs once a year when the new leaves emerge, and again after flowering to encourage them.

Bulbs that are evergreen. A note about bulbs that are nearly evergreen, such as amaryllis. Our heat and rainfall can be the death of many bulbs popular in more temperate zones. We see their pictures, but wet soils or hot summers make us grow them like annuals, if at all. On the other hand, there's amaryllis. We buy them dried out after their season in their native south Africa. That is why they bloom in December first, then get acclimated to our opposite season, and bloom in spring. They're evergreen in nature, by the way.

Bulbs as annuals. A particular group of bulbs is best grown here as annuals. Tulips are a good example. The bulb you buy blooms and dies, to be replaced in ideal conditions by a daughter bulb that grows over the summer, rests, sprouts and blooms the following year. Our summers are too hot for the daughter to develop the potential to flower, so if the tulips survive to the next year, flowers will be few even if the leaves come back up.

Bulbs to dig and store. Caladium and dahlia are bulbs that zone 8 gardeners (and some in very wet areas of Zone 9) dig up and store after their season finishes in the fall. Unlike tulips, these bulbs can be planted again next year with good results. Store them dry, in boxes or mesh bags, packed in dry material like cedar shavings.

Growing bulbs means getting in their groove, understanding that this group of plants has adapted into sort of an organic safety deposit box. Some grow leaves first, then flowers, then slowly die back and rest between seasons. Others bloom first, then leaf out, and later rest before new flowers appear. Both processes depend on the health of the bulb or the corm, rhizome, or tuber, which I fondly call faux bulbs. I try to honor the crown of perennials and embrace the thatch in my lawn, and always baby the bulbs. Notice I said that I try, as these babies are sometimes tougher than they look. I'll admit I've let bags of narcissus take a two-day ride around in the trunk and once left a gift of daylilies in a bushel basket for more than a month. Both are alive and well in my garden now, but didn't get off to a good start because I didn't use my own advice.

Bulb Tips

Buy the biggest bulbs you can find of whatever type you're planning to grow, then plant them pointy end or eyes up. If someone gives you small bulbs, plant them anyway, but have patience for their performance. And if you do plant caladiums upside down, they'll have more leaves, but they'll be smaller. (This last demonstration makes a great science project.)

Refrigerate tulip and hyacinth bulbs for eight weeks before planting, and get them in the ground by New Year's if at all possible. These two need a definite cold period for strong, tall stems, and full flowers. They are the only bulbs that routinely need refrigerating.

Bulbous plants will sometimes rot, especially rhizomes or tubers buried too deep in cold soil. Bulbs shipped by uncaring people will rot, too. I hardly ever say never, but I mean never buy bulbs that are soft, mushy, or papery, and if you order some that come that way, complain loudly. These are living things, after all.

Provide a well-drained soil (unless you're growing white spider lilies or other swamp denizens) and if you doubt its fertility, put a heaping teaspoon of a balanced granular formula into the hole below each bulb. Dig the hole, put in the fertilizer, refill with a bit of soil, then the bulb and more soil on top of that. The idea here is to put the fertilizer where the roots will be without burning the bottom of the bulb. Please do not use bone meal, as it takes a year to become available and has safety issues associated with its animal origins.

When planting a group of the same bulb, or an organized display, weed the area very well and set all the bulbs out where they will be planted before digging the holes or mulching. This way you can space them properly, and won't accidentally plant one on top of another.

Divide perennial bulbs by the same rules used for other perennials, but use extra caution not to cut into the bulbs. That usually means using a shovel rather than a fork and digging into the soil several inches away from the base of the plant. Lay the shovelful of soil and bulbs gently on the ground or a table. Use your fingers to encourage each bulb to separate from the mass with some roots attached. When the roots are impossibly dense, cut them apart, but do not cut into the bulbs. Trim leaves to two-thirds their height, and replant the bulbs at the same depth they were growing. Space for good air circulation and eventual size so the bulbs need not be traumatized by this process more often than every five years.

Remember that just as you feed the leaves and roots, the bulb or tuber or corm or rhizome will absorb some nutrients too, and sock them away. In a practical sense, it means using a flowering formula when new growth begins each year so there's plenty of phosphorus and potassium to keep them going. Their ability to store what they need to grow also means that if you don't feed them, they'll live on their own pretty well in many cases. Thus the lines of daffodils and spider lilies that bloom on old home sites. Nobody alive ever fed them, and they do fine: leaves grow, then transfer their nutrients into the fattened stem or root where next year's flower and leaves get their nutrition. That's how these magnificent plants do it.

Lawns

Lawns here in the Deep South are the warm season turf grasses: bermuda, zoysia, centipede, and St. Augustine. I like a lawn to walk on and sincerely appreciate turf's efficiency. It cleans the air and lowers the temperature over its surface in comparison to adjacent pavement by as much as 25 degrees. That means when it's hot enough to fry eggs on the sidewalk, the TV reporter sent out to prove it could cook standing barefooted on the lawn next to the walk!

Lawns are the subject of much debate about what care they need. But there's also plenty of talk about whether to have turf, or just mow what grows and hope it's green. The comic Alan King once had a routine about moving to suburbia. As a working comedian, he kept late hours and especially looked forward to sleeping in on the weekends after his shows. He regaled the audience with the antics of his neighbors. Each seemed set on mowing and edging his lawn louder and earlier than King could imagine in his worst nightmare. And this before the days of leaf blowers!

Most of us live somewhere between fanatically manicuring and completely shunning the turf grass in the yard. The keys to a quality lawn are full sun, soil that drains adequately, access to water and fertilizer, and a willingness to mow regularly. As the amount of sun decreases, the lawn's chances of success are compromised and your work is made harder.

Drainage. The importance of the soil's ability to use water effectively cannot be overstated, but there is another factor at work in lawns. The relationship of the turf to the rest of the property needs close attention, especially when putting in a new lawn or renovating an old one. Be sure the lawn slopes evenly and gently away from the house and other structures to move water away from them. If there are low spots or humps in the lawn's profile, they soon become puddles and dry spots. Hard to manage and difficult to mow, such areas soon become vulnerable to pests.

Grass types. Each of the turf grasses has its best use. **Bermuda grass** makes a resilient surface for children and dogs to romp on, but to get that tight, durable quality you must mow it regularly to about one inch high.

Zoysia is almost as good for foot traffic, grows a bit slower than bermuda, and has a lusher look when mowed regularly to about an inch and a half tall. But it can be unforgiving in drought and can be more difficult to resuscitate if it goes dormant from lack of water at midsummer.

Zoysia pales in the charm department next to **St. Augustine,** that queen of southern turf. Those wide blades and crayon green color evoke picnics on the lawn, and indeed, none is better for sitting or walking barefoot. St. Augustine doesn't just seem like a deeper cushion, it is one. It is mowed at about three inches. It is subject to fungus diseases, most often because the sunlight in the area is marginal, or because you overused nitrogen fertilizers in an attempt to get the grass to grow in less than ideal conditions.

Centipede grass has been touted as low maintenance; indeed it grows more slowly than the others and thus requires mowing less often to maintain its ideal height, two inches tall. Its slow nature sometimes frustrates gardeners, since the lawn often cannot outgrow its troubles the way the other grasses usually can.

Seed or Sod?

New lawns face their own demons, primarily our tendency to plant them at the wrong time. Sodding in summer means providing water every day, sometimes twice daily in dry, windy weather. Maybe worse, sod can rot if summer thunderstorms flood it before it has time to root into your soil. Spring and, believe it or not, autumn are less stressful times for installing the turf squares. Sod offers the instant gratification we all seek, and frankly is a good investment in the front yard and other high traffic areas. In less public areas, on larger properties, or in the name of economy, seeding is a fine option.

Hybrid bermuda grass is the most popularly seeded, sometimes in combination with the seeds of clumping carpet grass. Daily watering is crucial to the seedbed, too, which needs to be prepared even more carefully than you would do for sod. You'll often see hay spread over a newly seeded lawn to prevent erosion and camouflage the seeds from birds that will eat it. Sod and seed have their places, certainly, but when there is a mix of turf grasses and other plants, especially in the private areas of a property, I'm the first to agree you should mow what grows.

The Woody Trio: Trees, Shrubs, and Roses

Three of my plant groups are distinguished by their woody stems, which work almost the same way as green, herbaceous ones. But woody ornamental plants grow more slowly and problems can take much longer to become apparent, sometimes only when the plant is in serious trouble. Understanding the differences in how they grow can lead the gardener to give them what they need to be the stalwarts of your garden style that they should be.

Trees

Trees are more likely to outlive you than any other plant, and deserve their legacy status even if it can be frustrating to wait for them to grow. Most people consider a nice lawn and a big shade tree the hallmarks of a home's outdoor beauty and choosing it (or them) can be daunting because of their longevity. Tree choice isn't the same, blasé act as picking the color of this year's pansies. No matter how much you dislike that shade of purple, it'll be gone in a few months. Trees, though, deserve more thought than they often get, especially since few of us actually get to pick our trees. We inherit them in the same way we inherit the driveway and moving either just isn't practical.

Trees are deciduous, evergreen, or something in between. The few that kindly drop all their leaves all at once, like gingko, are the raker's dream. Otherwise, think harvest and put those leaves to their best use, compost. Evergreens and, more obviously, the in-betweens lose leaves, too, but not at such a rate that you notice. Famously, red oak belatedly drops its leaves in waves until just before the new growth comes on. You could go nuts trying to keep the area beneath it neatly raked! Live oaks' new growth pushes the old leaves off, so it is effectively evergreen, but drops plenty of leaves in an average year.

If I could wave a magic wand, or be granted one wish for rubbing a watering can, it would be this: everyone would know instantly the actual names of the

trees in their yard. With that one bit of information, the specific details for growing and maintaining these garden staples is at your beck and call. Growing trees obviously takes time, as well as soil the roots can use, water, and nutrients in adequate amounts. Since you will live with your trees for many years, it is especially important to prune and care for them while their limbs are still within your reach. Maintaining older trees includes protecting them from compaction or other intrusion into their root zones in addition to annual fertilizer applications and irrigation in dry years.

35

The structure of trees. The incredibly complex world of the cell is at its best in trees, and caring for them makes more sense if you know a bit about how the tree miraculously grows. Inside the bark of every woody stem, there is the **cambium** layer and then the **wood** of the tree. Cambium, literally 'change,' does exactly that when it differentiates the way its cells are arranged to create the plumbing of the plant, the **xylem** and **phloem**. These structures carry water and nutrients until xylem becomes wood and phloem ages into bark.

The cambium layer rests between them in woody plants and as long as it is alive, there can be growth. You've seen the results in cold-damaged shrubs. Though they look frozen, a simple scratch test reveals a green cambium with its promise for recovery underneath the bark. The mighty cambium is also responsible for the frozen shrubs that burst into bloom anyway, only to turn brown and die at midsummer. Look closely and you'll see split bark at the base of such shrubs, a sure sign that the cambium finally gave up the ghost. Sometimes, even then you can cut the shrub back and see some regrowth. It all depends on how the cambium does, and how well the growth process adapts to seasonal changes. You can see the results of this adaptation in tree rings, where the xylem cells that become wood are captured in annual rings. As the tree grows, some years are wetter, others drier, and the xylem cells grow thicker or thinner as a result, as can be seen by examining these rings in a cross section of the tree trunk.

Shrubs

Like trees, shrubs are woody plants. It is not height that distinguishes them from trees. They do not have a tree's classic trunk in most cases, and then only when fully mature. Instead, shrubs are noted for having a group of main woody stems, but their mature height ranges from six inches to well over 20 feet in some cases. Whether evergreen or deciduous types have been chosen, planting shrubs signals a decision in favor of permanence. Even in a container garden, annuals must be replaced and perennials moved out of sight when their season is done. But shrubs stay safely planted for years, lending continuity to any kind of garden.

Most of the questions about shrubs are about pruning, and those issues are addressed elsewhere in the book (see page 55). Beyond requiring trimming to curb their enthusiasm, shrubs need less from you than any other plant group except certain bulbs. Plant some shrubs, but think about this important limitation. The temptation of a bargain is mighty, especially for overgrown shrubs late in the season at the garden center. Potbound plants are always a bit awkward to deal with, but some types of potbound shrubs should be avoided. Every instinct says to slash through those roots so tightly wound, and plant. But first, consider that our soils are rife with pathogens hanging around just waiting for an opening into a root to rot it. By cutting through the roots of already vulnerable species or variety, you multiply the opportunities for fatal disease. Examples include holly, boxwood, gardenia, and banana, and if their soil is not very well drained, roses. To be on the safe side, when you do have to root prune any newly purchased shrub, do so. Then pot it up again until it has recovered before planting it in garden soil. Or go on and plant it, but water it in with a fungicide solution.

Roses

Roses are the symbols of love, alright, but what a lot of bunk there is out there about them! All roses are shrubs, regardless of how they are pruned. Yet they are a special class of shrubs to me because of the distinct ways the different types are treated in the garden. So long as you have a bit more than half a day of sun, (or dappled sun all day for a very few varieties) you can grow roses. Once again, a change in expectations may be necessary. If you are set on perfect, long-stemmed roses for the vase and flower show, hybrid teas are in your garden, but not mine. I admire your flowers, but I will grow any sort of rose, so long as it doesn't require regular spraying to prevent devastation from black spot fungus or insect pests. That leaves out virtually every hybrid tea.

When I first began collecting roses, it soon became obvious that there were some that tolerated the southern garden better than others. I wanted more of the ones that actually grew well as garden shrubs and that led to learning about their backgrounds as a way to predict garden behavior. Here are the roses that I grow.

Species roses: A tea rose (not a hybrid tea rose, but one of their parents) such as 'Aloha' has a very upright habit, strong canes and good flowers for cutting. 'Lady Banks', the once-blooming, nearly thornless star of the spring garden, also has an upright habit formed from a multitude of vigorous climbing canes.

Chinas: The first remontant or reblooming rose have neatly pointed leaves and a decidedly fruity fragrance. They are middle sized shrubs like 'Archduke Charles' and 'Butterfly Rose' (yellow, pink, crimson). They tolerate clay soil and southern heat. Prune only to remove old wood. By the way, there are so many of these Chinas that it's a wonder we grow anything else. Luckily, their children have some of the same fine qualities.

Bourbons: Crosses between China roses and the European roses bred from them, Bourbons such as 'Maggie' are noted for their rosy scent.

Polyanthas: These are crosses between China roses and Japanese roses of the late 19th century, and include 'The Fairy' and 'Clothilde Soupert'. The first may be the easiest of all roses to grow and the second is my favorite for its fragrance and soft pink color.

Floribundas: Tea species crossed with polyantha such as 'Nearly Wild', a very old rose, and 'Julia Child,' a 21st century introduction. Did I mention that rose breeding is an ancient art and a vital part of today's pursuit of the perfect rose, too?

Noisettes: Bred in Charleston for erect form and tolerance of heat and clay soils. Flowers are held in huge, drooping clusters and noted for frequent reblooming. Noisettes include 'Natchitoches Noisette' and 'Lamarque'.

Modern: Today, breeding focuses on garden performance, and there are some lovely, reliable roses that deserve your attention. The 'Meidiland' group deserves more attention than it gets, as do some of the David Austin roses. The 'Knockout' series has given us roses that are not only easy to grow, but easy for growers to propagate, so they're widely available.

Charming as they are, roses are the fussy maiden aunts of the garden. They dislike wet feet and wear flowery hats with class. Like other shrubs, they benefit greatly from a compost blanket in early spring. Unlike most others, roses are rather free spenders, able to use up generous amounts of water and fertilizer. To gain superior drainage, both water and air, roses are often planted in raised beds or on terraces within borders.

Edibles: What's for Dinner

More and more, people are growing things to eat at home. The strongest emphasis is certainly on herbs, followed by fruits and vegetables. This interest is a revival for some, who grew up with a vegetable garden or a fig tree by the garage. But the larger number find themselves in new territory, taking on a more personal attitude towards what's for dinner in this century. While there is no real difference in their

flat-leaved parsley

parts or growth processes, edibles fall into two overall categories, vegetables and fruits. Most vegetables and their partner, herbs, are annual or perennial. There are exceptions such as the woody bay tree and shrubby rosemary.

Eat Your Veggies

It's quite possible that every annual vegetable known to humans can grow at some time of the year in the South. Note the number of days a particular variety takes to produce, then look at your calendar to find the number of days with weather that suits the plant you want to grow.

beet

Perennial vegetables such as asparagus and horseradish are more problematic. Raised beds help solve the need for deep root zones, and old window screens can offer shade from summer's heat, and freeze protection is possible. But rhubarb or rutabaga? Somebody in the South grows them all plus kohlrabi and every melon known. Find a few superior catalogs and web sites and read them, seeking varieties bred for short seasons, anything noted for heat tolerance, and southern heirlooms. If you are serious about growing more than basil and tomatoes, learn to grow from seed so you have access to dozens if not hundreds of varieties. Universally, gardeners who sow their own exude a quietly smug attitude, especially when we show off a favorite that is only available from seed. Join us! For more how-to, see the section about propagation which begins on page 43.

My fab five. Here are my fab five, non-tomato veggies for the home garden. I nominate these for easy growing and amazing taste you can't get at the store. The second criteria explains why squash, watermelon, and sweet corn are not on this list. For me at least, those are best bought at the local farmer's market.

> **beans, green and yellow wax.** Of course, there are plenty of green beans to be had, but only in my home garden can I grow purple and yellow beans. No child or finicky friend can resist the truly oddball, so tempt that curiosity!

> **peppers, sweet and hot.** I do not grow bell peppers and hardly eat them at all, but sweet banana and pepperoncini are in my garden every year, plus at least four hot peppers. I grow Tabasco and whatever else strikes my fancy at seed planting time.

> **lettuces, spinach, greens of all sorts.** You need to eat more of these than you do, so grow a bed or box full every fall. Take a tip from truck farmers and build a shaded hoop structure to extend the greens season by several weeks or even months. The potential twelve month growing

39

season can become reality more easily if you prepare to protect your plants from extremes at both ends of the thermometer. At the same time, you'll exclude the majority of pests, too.

Brussels sprouts. Until you've grown 'em, you don't know what you're missing.

beets. Yes, beets make my short list. I was full grown before anyone ever gave me a fresh, steamed plate of beets and you may never have had the pleasure. Besides, growing beets gives you an excuse to dig a very deep bed capable of growing those roots. That'll improve your chances with carrots and turnips, too.

Herbs for all Seasons

Herbs can be divided into annual and perennial, but also into those best suited for each different season. You can grow them all in beds and containers, and I suggest the latter if your soil is not very well drained. It is important to shop locally when buying herb plants. Each area has its favorites, and the best adapted selections often come from the divisions of a neighbor's herbs.

Annual herbs for spring and summer. Basil and borage are easy. Parsley and dill can make it if planted in very early spring.

Annual herbs to grow over winter. Parsley, cilantro, dill, fennel, garlic, onions for bulbs and scallions, multiplying onions, and shallots.

Perennial herbs for beds. Oregano, onion and garlic chives (may reseed, too), tarragon, Mexican mint marigold (nice flavor substitute in regions where French tarragon is finicky), mints, winter savory, rue, and pennyroyal.

Perennial perhaps, perhaps not. Certain plants grown as perennials don't last forever! When in doubt, grow in a container or as an annual in the bed. Move the pots indoors, into your greenhouse, or a cold frame whenever necessary. The greatest advantage to growing all the herbs in pots is twofold. Cold, wet soil is no longer a threat to delicate root systems, and you can put the plants close at hand. Each fall I plant a big shallow bowl-shaped pot with a few lettuces, parsley, a few onion sets, sage, and thyme. The herb garden sits outside the kitchen door, readily accessible when the garden is wet and the day is dreary. In truly inclement weather, I haul it in to the kitchen.

Other sometimes perennials include sage and thyme (don't forget the creeping one), lemongrass, edible ginger, bay tree, rosemary (most likely to be perennial), and the beautifully scented pineapple sage.

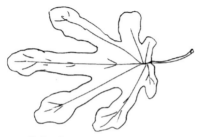

figleaf

Berries, Fruits and Nuts

Including berries, fruiting plants can be **annual** (strawberries except everbearing types), **perennial** (blackberry), **shrubby** like blueberry, or true **trees**. The list of fruits and nuts that it is possible to grow is long but not all the choices are reasonable. Some, like older pecan varieties and most peaches, demand strict spray regimens to fend off entirely predictable pest problems. There are reports of peach trees that bear without care, and I strongly suggest you propagate any such tree you come across.

Locally adapted specimens deserve more attention for their own goodness and for the material and insights they offer to plant breeders. Those breeders are responsible for the improved varieties we grow, and nowhere is that more obvious than in fruit. **Fig** is the poster child of their work, with new releases going far beyond last century's great figs to beat them with greater abundance and better growing habits. One fig tree is almost always enough for the average family. It is a notable exception to my rule of fruit: plant two of every fruit to improve pollination and harvest potential. Two varieties are not always necessary, but are highly recommended for many favorites to do their best, including plums, persimmons, apples, and pears.

The list of fruits that can easily be grown in the garden at home includes those that are native and/or well-adapted to the South. Most often, this last phrase means a plant has few pests and can tolerate humid soil. Even so, we are able to grow a wider range of fruits and nuts than other regions, and cherish them. Pomegranates, for example, have been around for years, and are gaining favor among backyard orchardists annually for their health benefits.

Recent efforts to cultivate the native (and nearly lost) black walnut may mean they will return in all their majesty to our forests.

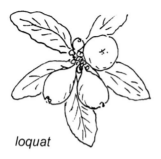

loquat

Subtropicals. The farther south you travel, the better conditions are for the subtropical delights. Loquat, citrus (except kumquat and satsuma citrus types which are hardier), and pineapple guava will grow, but may not bear in cooler areas unless grown in containers and/or protected from late spring freezes.

Whatever fruit, nut, or berry you decide to grow, get ahead of the curve by learning all you can about it before you plant a new one or prune an inherited one. If you have the room, make room for our native paw paw trees. They look tropical, with huge leaves that rival bigleaf magnolia, and the luscious yellow fruit may inspire you to pick some up, if not to put them in your pocket. Even if you don't eat the fruit, plant at least one of these and give the birds and squirrels a real treat.

By the way, if anyone ever offers you fresh pear pie that involves Ritz cracker crumbs, ask for a second helping. You'll want it, and get the recipe so I can have it.

Fig. My family always had fig preserves and pear preserves ready to serve with toast in the morning, cornbread at dinner, and biscuits for supper. The positive spin on this carbo-sugar diet is that we ate our largest meal at noon, and so it was called dinner. That gave us all day to work off what we ate, with a smaller supper at night. These days we eat no more than twice a day, much less bread, and fresh figs in season. Tastes have changed, but so have figs.

There are at least six figs that will grow where you live, so get yourself to the garden center and buy one or two for different tastes and harvest times.

Plant figs in a sunny spot with plenty of room around it. Figs have a shallow, wide root system that needs mulch on it all year and a soil rich in organic matter. Dig a hole wider than deep and amend it with compost, leaf mold, aged manure, and ground bark, too, if the native soil is very heavy.

Work the mulch into the soil around figs as it decays and replace it. Water weekly in dry seasons, especially if fruit is present. Fertilize young trees with a complete formula when new growth emerges and again at midsummer. Established figs can be fertilized in spring with the same complete formula, after pruning with organic nitrogen, or not at all if its growth and production suit you.

Prune figs in winter, or not at all, and plant them then, too. After planting a new tree, prune it as much as needed to establish a strong trunk and branches. Take a few inches off all over a young tree to stimulate new growth and shape the tree.

Approach an old fig with respect. If it hasn't been pruned in years, you may delay the crop by cutting too drastically. To rejuvenate, or control the height so you can pick the fruit, you can cut off up to one fourth of the canopy at a time.

Blueberry. The ideal shrub may be the blueberry. A neat habit, sweet flowers, and red fall color that makes it glow recommend blueberry even to those not enamored with the fruit. The birds will thank you to leave some for them, but I suggest netting the bushes as soon as ripening begins so you get your share first.

If you can grow azaleas and have a couple more hours of sun than they need, you can grow blueberries. Both thrive in acid soil that is well-drained and watered regularly, surrounded by mulch and pruned annually. Choose a locally favored variety. In general, for blueberries, cut back the bushes after the fruiting has finished to shape them and keep next year's fruit within reach. (Prune azaleas within one month after flowering.) Fertilize young blueberry plants with a complete formula in spring and after fruiting. Once the berries are established and fruiting well, fertilize after summer pruning.

Anywhere in our region where the soil pH is lower than 6.0, a native blueberry (Vaccinum species) can be found. Two types dominate garden culture, Southern highbush and rabbiteye. One is favored over the other in many localities, although generally the latter is more heat tolerant. Stick with the varieties recommended by the nearest cooperative extension or blueberry grower associations and you'll have fine crops.

Strawberries are hugely popular, but most taste like cardboard to me because I have eaten homegrown strawberries all my life. Experienced gardeners and those in less humid places grow the everbearing sort, but in my garden they seem to be spider mite nests in summer. I keep trying, though, and in the meantime, grow the annual strawberries in winter. Look for the plants in fall alongside the lettuces at garden centers and plant about two dozen in a bed spaced six to eight inche apart. Be sure the soil is rich and drains well. Fertilize as often as you do the overwintering annuals such as pansies. Many gardeners mulch strawberries with hay so when the fruit comes on in spring it stays above the often wet ground. Use what you have, but do mulch them to keep the fruit clean.

Propagation

Smarter sowing and growing, that's propagation. When you like a plant, you want more of it. It's simple and can be basic, but the word propagation seems to scare some people. Any time you plant a seed, pinch a stem and stick it in a glass of water, or dig up a crowded perennial and separate it before replanting, you're propagating plants and should be proud of it.

What roots when depends on the plant's growth habit and the part in question. Plenty of scholarly articles and garden lore alike delve into the specifics, but your knowledge of how the plant grows means more in the real world.

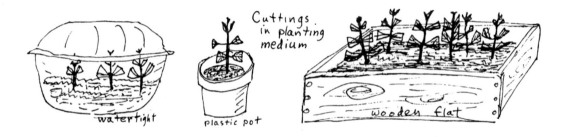

watertight   Cuttings in planting medium   plastic pot   wooden flat

Rooting woody plants

Every piece of woody stem is in one condition or another, and some kinds of plants root better in one state than the other. New growth bends easily onto itself and so is called **soft wood**. It is ideal for rooting shrubs that become twiggy or woody early in the season. As the new growth becomes woody, it reaches a stage known as **semi-hard wood.** The new stem will bend, but not as easily as when it was soft, and it does not snap readily. Both soft and semi-hard cuttings root best in small pots or flats filled with a mix of potting soil and finely ground bark. The idea is to keep the media moist enough to sustain the bare wood without rotting it before roots develop. Cuttings made in spring and summer from these woods benefit from natural humidity. They can usually be left outdoors in the shade to root without needing a mist system commonly found in greenhouses and arid climates. Still, I keep a spray bottle nearby and mist the plants on hot days. In about two weeks, most cuttings will begin to root, indicated by the resistance they offer to your gentle tug. Shrubs that root well from soft wood include abelia, maple, bottlebrush, witch hazel, magnolia, althea, and blueberry.

The list of those that root best from semi-hard wood is extensive, but some of my favorites in the large group are crepe myrtle, butterfly bush, camellia, gardenia, azalea, rhododendron, sweet shrub, and rose. Exactly when the wood is ready varies by the date when new growth begins for the current season, but is about eight weeks after that. Consider the two most popular camellias as an example: sasanqua ends its bloom in fall and may begin growing before the japonicas finish blooming, or may not. It isn't when the shrub blooms, but when it begins to grow that determines when the wood begins to harden. Azaleas may not flower at all for one reason or another, yet the new shoots will often emerge on time anyway.

Hardwood cuttings are the mature wood of late summer and fall, and unlike the other two kinds, do not root only from tip cuttings. Rather, cut straight stems from the current year's growth, clip off the tip if rooting a deciduous shrub, and trim to three or four nodes per cutting. Stick a bunch of these cuttings into a mix of sand and compost that you have watered once. Protect from freezing during the winter, but leave the pot outside in a cold frame, an unheated greenhouse, or a shed. Deciduous shrubs that root from hard wood include barberry, dogwood, deutzia, eleagnus, euonymus, forsythia, St. John's wort, kerria, ligustrum, mock orange, photinia, coral and other honeysuckles, spirea, viburnum, chaste tree, wiegela, and rose.

Evergreen shrubs will root better with a mist system, but you can enclose a pot of these cuttings in a plastic cloche with bottom heat. The power of a professional quality, horticultural, waterproof heat source cannot be under-stated. UL-listed and available at greenhouse and garden retailers, you will choose between a heating cable in a bed of sand or a heating mat. Pots or flats sit on top of either heat source to warm their soil and promote rooting or seed germination. Open the chamber several times daily to ventilate and provide air exchange, and to mist by hand. Evergreen shrubs that root from hard wood include aucuba, boxwood, holly, Indian hawthorne, and Virginia sweetspire.

One of the best reasons to be a gardener is that there is something to propagate every month of the year. These lists aside, try rooting cuttings when you have the time or find yourself with prunings too healthy to compost or toss out. When someone gifts you with a potted shrub, a houseplant outgrows its space, or a loved one moves and leaves behind a plant you cherish, take cuttings. If you fear a favorite plant is dying, take a cutting regardless of the season. It might root, and that's enough for me.

Should you use powdered rooting hormone? It's a good idea for cut woody stems and I use it when I remember that it's in the greenhouse. To use it efficiently, shake a little pile onto a paper towel, then roll the cut stem in it. Don't 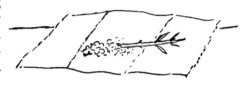 pour leftover powder back in with the rest because when you take it out of the container it gets contaminated and could ruin the whole batch.

Layering. Another way to root many shrubs and even some trees is to layer their lowest branches. The idea here is that you encourage roots to sprout from a stem still attached to the mother plant, using a natural life support system. Dig a shallow trench under a low limb and bury part of it. Use a brick or board to weigh it down if necessary, and be sure a few green leaves and a bit of stem stick out of the trench on the end away from the mother plant. To stimulate rooting it  helps to scratch the bark of the underground part. If you do layering like this in spring, most layers will be rooted and start to grow a bit by fall. Sometimes you can find naturally occurring layers under azaleas and other shrubs. When the layer is well rooted, cut the stem behind the trench, dig it up along with its green top, and plant it where you want it to grow.

Rooting Green-Stemmed Plants

Besides woody plants, gardeners root green-stemmed plants of other sorts. Sometimes it starts because a coleus or mint tries to bloom, and you pinch off the flower and a couple of leaf sets. You wander back in the house and wonder if it would root in a glass of water. It does, if you pluck the flower off, and soon your windowsill is a maze of bottles and jars filled with this and that. Some that obviously should root, don't, like a piece of pothos ivy that achieved nothing after two months on my sill. A few drops of fertilizer in the water didn't help and it landed in the trash. Others that shouldn't take root, such as cut flower roses, somehow manage to do so for some people. My advice is still to avoid taking cuttings from stems in bloom or bud, as the biochemistry goes against its success. I also advise rooting woody plants like roses in soil, not water, but please, at least clip the flower off the cutting when you ignore me.

In fact, as soon as cuttings started in water develop roots, its time to pot them up unless you intend growing lucky bamboo or a Chinese evergreen in a brandy snifter with a beta fish swimming beneath. This book does not address hydroponics, but growing in water or nutrient solutions is definitely workable in many situations. Classrooms and other congregate settings may not have space or allow much soil indoors for health reasons, but a hydroponic garden is always an option there, too.

You can root the same herbaceous plants in a well-drained potting mix as in water, and many more types that would rot in constantly moist conditions. Rooting green cuttings is like rooting soft and semi hard wood cuttings, but with two important differences. First, the soil can be a mix of potting soil and compost with a little sand or bark added if the mix seems too wet. Second, green plants rapidly lose water through their leaves and can wilt fatally before they root. It's often a good idea to pre-empt this problem by cutting off half of each leaf, not half the leaves, to reduce the surface area that must be supported by the rootless stem. For the same reason, keep cuttings out of drying wind and direct sun. Remarkably, the efficient cellular structure in green stems can keep the top growth hydrated and generate roots simultaneously, with a bit of help from you.

**Easy-To-Root Herbaceous Plants**	_**Easy-to-root Woody Plants**_
coleus	rose
philodendron	azalea
geranium (keep 'em on the dry side)	fig
tomatoes (from suckers)	crepe myrtle
mint	gardenia
lantana	hibiscus

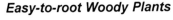

Division: Divide to Conquer

In between the woody plants and the green stemmed ones are the **perennials**. This group of plants can be divided for propagation. Many can be grown from seed and green cuttings as well, and from offsets, the little plants that sprout up around an established perennial. But the primary method of increasing perennials is by division, also called digging and dividing.

The essence of plant division is to get plantable pieces, each with a bit of the three parts of a perennial: the top growth (usually green but not always), the crown (the sometimes woody center), and the root, without damaging their growing points. The tools of this task can include trowel, shovels, hand cultivator, digging fork, clippers, and saws. Occasionally it's helpful to have a lopper and chainsaw nearby. The idea is to get the plant out of the ground entirely, then cut it into pieces with as little ado as possible. Pulling and hacking are out, neatly slicing is in because it creates less trauma and so less transplant shock.

The pieces may be replanted in the garden or potted up and grown in a nursery area. While the plant is out of the ground, take the time to rework the soil where it grew by adding organic matter or grit mix as needed to improve its fertility and drainage. As described in the section on growing perennials, divide your plants when growth is so thick it stops their flowering.

bow rake

Seedwise

There is a remarkable amount of wildly general information about starting seeds in garden books and on seed packs. According to some instructions, you can plant whatever it is in the garden or start it ahead for transplant with the same results. That is not always so, as most everyone learns the first time they plant lettuce or impatiens from seed. Those tiny devils get lost in the cracks of the soil, or sprout in a clump too thick to thin. Sadly, the detailed instructions given for some seeds can be daunting. How can I possibly provide a shredded sphagnum moss bed at a constant 70 degrees in bright but not direct light? The seeds sit in the drawer, and if I have to have it, I buy a plant. As with most things, I approach seeds somewhere in the middle of the two extremes. I recognize that there are plants like moonflowers and sunflowers, standard zinnias and fall spinach that I (and most gardeners) find impossible to transplant and that others including most vegetables are hard to find as plants. Thus motivated, here are my notes on growing from seed:

Do yourself a favor and get a **seed-starting setup.** Find a space in your house for an energy-saving, state-of-the-art light fixture with trays and perhaps a plastic hood. Then start playing with seeds. Preferably you'll put it in front of a window, but since the better models are self-contained, you can put it on top of the sewing machine cabinet if necessary.

47

Discover the world of **peat planters.** When the seedlings make the move to the garden, these handy cups and pellets can be planted in toto, reducing transplant shock. Whether it is under lights or on the porch outside, put the pellets or cups in a plastic flat. Fill the cups with sterile seed starting mix, water them once, and plant. Soak the pellets as directed and plant promptly.

Water seedlings by adding water to a tray below them so the pots or pellets or cellpaks can take up water routinely, as needed. This practice helps prevent fungus diseases encouraged by wet leaves.

Set up a **bottom heat system** (cable or mat) to warm the soil below peppers and other heat loving plants.

Make friends with your **garden rake** to plant seeds outdoors. Not a leaf rake, this one has hard tines about three inches long on a straight shaft. After you have turned the soil, turn the shovel over and chop it into smaller clumps that you can rake smooth. Really smooth, and yes, this applies to seeding lawns, too.

Small seeds. If the seed are small, or the bed less than terrific due to very wet or dry conditions, top the seed bed with half an inch of compost mixed with potting soil and plant into that.

Water seed beds gently, with a fan nozzle on the hose or a rose head watering can. Keep the bed moist until the seed sprout, letting it dry out just slightly between waterings. Seed must have good contact with the soil and then be able to absorb water to sprout. If you can check it daily, lay a board on top of the seed bed to keep it from drying out. You must remove it as soon as the first sprout breaks the soil.

Thin to win. Read the seed packet for proper spacing and make it so if you want plants that perform optimally with good growth and thick stems. I keep a yardstick and a foot ruler handy and actually measure these things. Even if I crowd them a bit anyway, I know what I should have done.

Chapter 3. Southern Growing Strategies

Every living thing has limiting factors. Some stress is okay and sometimes it's very desirable, like when water is withheld from plants like Christmas cactus to trigger flowering. But serious stress involving even one factor can have consequences that domino out of control. For me, it's the dinner dilemma. If I have to shop, cook, and clean up all for the same meal, I'm a wreck. If I have to do two out of three, I'm okay, but make me do all of them in one fell swoop after a full day of work, and you may as well put me to bed without eating a bite. For plants, the Big Three are the **essential growth factors**, light, water (both irrigation and humidity), and nutrition. When all three come together in harmony with the plant's needs, it responds well, as I do when someone else offers to clean up after I've shopped and cooked. When one limiting factor is seriously out of whack though, the others can't make up for it.

Managing Water, Sunlight And Fertilizer. Think of light, water, and nutrition as the equal arms on a triangle. Each is equally important for thrifty plant growth, but how strict and how tolerant each will be depends on the plant in question. Plants that can grow in a variety of conditions are often called forgiving or bulletproof. The arms of their triangles can stretch in any direction and far from the comfortable ideal, yet they grow on. Most of the plants we commonly grow can be described as somewhat tolerant. That's a nice way to say that the plants that usually survive in our gardens can take the conditions we provide, and we generally keep water, light, and nutrition within tolerances for them. Any one of those can be the limiting factor that keeps your lawn in stress if it gets way out of tolerable conditions. No single factor has to be perfect, but all must be within acceptable limits. The triangle can stretch away from equilateral, but your crepe myrtle won't bloom if any one factor gets too far out of whack.

light   water

nutrition

Finally, its important to look at all the factors as you gauge what to address in treating a sick plant, and a combination of stressors does add up. If I am that weeping fig we all have, and I have to live with no light, lots of water, and a place in the house directly under a heater vent, all the fertilizer in the world won't help. When you wonder what is wrong with any plant, know that there is too much stress on the triangle of essential plant growth factors. Figure out what the plant needs that it's not getting, shift the balance, and voila! Better growth and a happier gardener. Here is how you can control the factors and achieve better plant health:

The Factor of Light

Light comes from the sun and artificial sources, and it may shine directly on plants or be shaded in some degree by structures and larger plants.

49

Consider first what the sun does at your house, the direction it travels over your garden space. That may be the yard, the deck, patio, or balcony, but if it there is any sun at all, figure out when and where it shines. These observations may be helpful as you decide which areas will provide which plants with en   ̈ght to grow without stress.

The most sun usually reaches your garden on the south and west sic   king it ideal for plants like succulents and Mediterranean natives that lo   it and sunlight. Think salvias, gaillardia, rosemary, yucca, flax, and annual   rs like zinnia, moss rose, and portulaca.

Traditionally, **the least light** reaches your garden on the north side, the most heat on the west. Reflected heat from concrete or other structures can increase the temperature in any microclimate, a plus in some circumstances.

East and south are considered the best light exposures. Almost anything can grow with half a day or more of this light, from roses and lawn grasses to oak trees and hydrangeas.

The minimum light needed to grow plants is about the same illumination it takes to read a newspaper without squinting.

When the level of light is a stress factor, plants show predictable reactions. In low light you may see paleness, stretched or weak stems, no new leaves, and no flowers. In overly high light, the leaves of plants are sunburned: bleached pale, even white, with short internodes (stem on far right).

Other lights to love. The light that streams into a greenhouse in winter, particularly a glass house, is wonderful. The greenhouse effect has gotten so much bad press on the global scale, it's important to remember its warming and brightening effects on a winter day, too.

By concentrating the sun's rays, the glass or other covering works like a lens to focus it. Plants and people benefit. I lined the west wall of my greenhouse with big black pots full of concrete rubble to capture the sun's heat during the day. It is a simple passive solar system, where the built up heat releases at night. Not the fanciest or most efficient by any means, this simple use of the sun saves me hundreds of dollars annually in heating costs.

I do not maintain a tropical greenhouse, but what I call a holding house where tropicals can survive and woody plants are ecstatic. When you think about a place to protect and grow plants, remember that a greenhouse is any structure that is covered, regardless of its size, material, or design.

When there's not enough light outside, you can thin a tree's canopy or cut the tree down, replace a solid wood fence with chain link, or hang plants from tree limbs to catch some sun. Indoors, there are artificial light sources that provide a full spectrum of light. Sold under various names, these lights come with their own fixtures or as bulbs, in tabletop and spotlight designs. Traditional houseplants grown for their leaves may find a suitable spot to exist in your home, but they will actually grow if you give them additional light. Flowering plants and a host of succulents cannot do their best without it, and having it enables you to hold plants and grow cuttings from the garden as well as start seeds.

⬤ Water and Humidity

I treat water and humidity as one factor here because soil, leaf, and air moisture are all involved and must be in balance for plants to grow up to their potential. Irrigation, whether achieved through an in-ground system or above ground methods means soaking long enough for water to percolate into the soil. How fast you apply it is the rate. In an efficient system, ample water is delivered in as short a time as possible without puddling or runoff.

When too much water reaches garden soil too quickly, plants may wilt because their roots become saturated. They do not recover despite watering. Entire leaves may yellow all over the plant, or they may become mushy and slide off their stems. Usually plants recover as the soil dries, but too much too soon for too long can cause plant death when the water factor becomes a serious source of stress.

If you are watering at too slow a rate or for too short a time, the soil becomes or stays crusty even under mulch. When too little water is the stressor, many plants simply stop growing. Other, more serious drought symptoms include leaves that pale or that wilt and recover when irrigated. Finally, when drought stress is too much, the plant succumbs.

Water in the air is called humidity, and except for indoors, we have almost no control over it. Even in coastal areas we can't always get much of a breeze. Our naturally moisture-rich air can hold still better than anything except rocks. Dense, water-laden air conditions favor the growth and expansion of plenty of pest franchises but you can stop them by selecting resistant varieties and planting at the recommended spacing. When you look at crowded gardens or pictures of them, remember that such displays are actually a set, dressed for you or the camera to see. In the real world, spacing for good air circulation makes sense because it gives you healthy plants.

Fertilizer or Nutrition

Much is written about fertilizer but what you need to know to use it successfully is really quite brief. What is in the product you choose matters much more than the numbers on any one label. **Nitrogen, Phosphorus, and Potassium** (N, P, and K on product labels and chemical element charts) are The Big Three, needed in larger amounts than any others.

What Causes Leaves to Turn Yellow?

Nitrogen deficiency often shows itself when the older leaves usually lower down on the plant turn yellow. They are sacrificing themselves (and their chlorophyll) so the rest of the plant has enough nitrogen to sustain itself until you remember to fertilize.

Root rot pathogens clog up the plant's plumbing, invading the vascular system to deprive it of the ability to transport water and nutrients. The leaves don't get what they need, stop making chlorophyll, and turn yellow. Usually this condition happens first to older leaves, closer in to the main branches or trunk, but all up and down the plant.

Transplant shock turns leaves yellow soon after planting when the roots are traumatized and cannot recover quickly enough. Cutting back new transplants helps reduce the shock, as does watering in with a dilute fertilizer solution or a starter solution.

They're needed for thrifty plant growth. When you peruse the products available, your head can swim. Remember this: **nitrogen** is essential to shoots and leaves. It gets used up faster than other elements because it is very water soluble, and contributes directly to the flowering and fruiting process unless there's too much of it. For example, lawns over fertilized with nitrogen will more readily express brown patch fungus disease. Annual flowers and vegetables disappoint by growing huge plants that do not bear flowers or fruit.

Phosphorus and **potassium** are responsible for, among other things, strengthening cell walls, making minor elements available, and delivering on the promise of strong roots, full flowers, sumptuous fruit, and viable seed. Both are more persistent in the root zone than nitrogen, and phosphorus is capable of binding to iron in the soil. As more fertilizer is applied, either routinely or to address yellowing, toxic amounts of phosphorus can build up even as the plants look undernourished. When phosphorus and iron are bound to each other, neither contributes to plant growth as it should, and iron chlorosis can develop. That condition can express itself in leaves that are yellow between the veins, which stay green. Iron deficiency can also be seen in centipede grass when it is over fertilized with phosphorus. Its partner, potassium, is necessary in amounts second only to nitrogen and plays a huge role in keeping the plant's internal chemistry lab humming along.

Minor elements are also necessary for plant growth, but in tiny amounts compared to the big three. If you have ever tried to grow turnips or carrots and failed to get these edible roots despite excellently well-drained soil, a lack of minor elements might be to blame. Clay soils usually have plenty of all the minors, but if you are wondering, get the soil tested, or read the labels of fertilizers and soils you are adding to be sure they are complete formulas.

Using fertilizer. Here's my mantra: feed the soil, then feed the plants. In adding fertilizer to the soil in a new bed, take note of the amount of nitrogen already there via organic matters. Decomposition concentrates this precious element and water releases it into the soil. Manures are strong nitrogen sources. If you use them, go lightly with other nitrogens, whether incorporated into the soil or used on the plants. The good news is that if you suspect an overabundance of nitrogen, copious amounts of water will usually dilute it or at least wash it out of the plant's root zone. I like to add a little bit of ground phosphate rock and wood ash to provide phosphorus to new beds. In fact, except for beds containing truly acid loving plants (azalea, camellia, holly, blueberry) you can recycle fireplace ashes into any part of the garden. Use no more than half an inch each year on lawns.

The compost blanket described previously forms a bridge between soil and plant nutrition needs. It provides the big three nutrients in discrete amounts at the same time it adds organic matter to the soil. When it comes to fertilizing the plants, over the years I have used just about anything you have ever seen on a shelf. I've employed elementals, completes, balanced, and plenty of specialty products, both organic and chemical-based. The organics win every time in my garden for efficacy and results in plant performance.

Thrift: Garden Economics

Thrift is not just a little perennial plant which blooms wildly in hot pink explosions each spring. 'Thrift' also defines the desired growth habit of healthy plants. It takes good soil, adequate water, fertilizer, and light to grow plants, but deciding where to put them is another important choice gardeners make every day. Like choosing where to put a new storefront, deciding where to put plants within your garden is all about location and amenities.

Microzones. Your garden likely has four microzones, described relative to each other. A given space may be wet and sunny, wet and shady, dry and sunny, or dry and shady. Yes, dappled shade can be both wet and dry, but areas within that environment are usually one or another. Certainly seasons can be dry or

Fertilizer Words

Complete—one with some of each of the three major elements, N, P, & K

Balanced—one with equal amounts of the three major elements, N, P, & K

Specialty—one formulated for a particular plant or use, such as lawns or trees

Elemental —one with singular element, such as ground phosphate

Trace or Minor—one with the elements needed in tiny amounts

wet, but the gardener has some control over applied water when rainfall is inadequate.

Drought is a huge issue in large areas of the south, but just when we get used to growing drought-loving succulents and leaving the windows rolled down, rain sets in. Then we must dig ditches just to get to the flooded garden out back. Even so, understanding that different areas have basically different conditions can guide you to smarter plant choices and inspire you to create new zones in the garden.

It sounds easy: Match the plant's needs with conditions you can provide and you will grow great plants. It's easier if you remember the phrase 'within tolerance.' Remember the image of the triangle of plant growth factors and imagine yourself juggling them. Nothing fancy; just keeping each factor within the space you control. The result will be thrifty growth: steady, sturdy progression of stems and leaves, producing good color and predictable performance in flowers and fruit.

My list of top ten cultural practices to encourage thrifty growth includes an extra (lagniappe) tip. There is more about these methods elsewhere in the book.

1. Learn about varieties and shop smart. If the tag doesn't tell you, ask.

2. Know your microzones to know if that great looking plant has a chance in your garden

3. Be sure your soil drains before you plant. If unsure, do the dig a hole test. Fill your planting hole with water and check to be sure it percolates for at least 5 minutes and no more than 30.

4. Walk your garden every day. It's good for you, and is the staple of integrated pest management. Little problems can grow quickly and early intervention is always more successful when dealing with pests.

5. Deadhead flowers whether you expect the plant to rebloom or not. You'll encourage new growth and prevent fungus infections arising from fallen blooms such as petal blight in camellias.

6. Mulch in moderation. Two inches of organic matter is adequate, one is plenty for dry gardens or around trees. Three and four inches is a waste of mulch, and may absorb water intended for the soil below.

7. Whether you do or whether you don't dust or spray, learn to recognize and manage insects. More on this in the next chapter.

8. Clean your tools. Clean blades don't spread disease. Mix a 1:10 solution of bleach and water to dip cutting blades (hand shears, loppers, saws) between branches and between bushes. This is especially important when dealing with fireblight on Bradford and other pears. Failure to disinfect the blades after pruning a diseased tree can spread the disease to susceptible but uninfected plants. Blast the lawnmower deck with a strong stream of water between cuttings.

9. Plant and prune for good air circulation. Resist the sometimes overwhelming temptation to mimic magazine layouts that show plants cheek by jowl, a fully mature looking landscape no matter its age.

10. Set up systems to water and fertilize to avoid stressing plants with your forgetful habits. A good rule of thumb is that if plants look pale and wilt easily, you're late on fertilizer. When you walk across the lawn and the grass crunches at your step, you're several days late on watering.

11. When you've done your best, and a plant just won't perform, dig it up. You can choose whether to trash it, compost it, pot it up, replant it in another microzone, or give it to someone you dislike.

Pruning: Shear Fear

Too many gardeners let a timid spirit keep them from growing the most beautiful plants they could have. I call it prunophobia, or shear fear. Sometimes it's because of a bad experience, like a plant that died after you pruned it. Even though the effect (a dead plant) was not likely brought on by the cause you identify (your pruning), your confidence is shattered. So you stop pruning. Azaleas grow huge, perennials seed all over the place, trees look lopsided, and the pear tree quits bearing. It's so sad to have that nice yard look like the set of a horror movie, with your house all but hidden behind menacing horticulture.

 There are other reasons people don't prune. You've heard that if you prune at the wrong time of year, flowering shrubs won't bloom. That's true. Or a neighbor seems to spend all his time clipping something to no apparent result, so you figure it's a waste of time. Sometimes that's true, too, unless the neighbor has a very formal style garden that needs frequent pruning to maintain its consistent good looks. Other plants just never seem to be at the right stage for the pruning, such as vitex and butterfly bush, although it is clear that they need it at some point.

The cure for shear fear is already in your hands. I once took a job pruning 50 Formosa azaleas because I was young and stupid. The onerous task was to rejuvenate them, which means removing the tallest, fattest stems all the way to the ground. At times that week I despaired of ever finishing, much less calling the job a success, but I got it done. The next year, I went back and crowed at their beauty and I had helped! That's how we get over the fear of pruning: inform yourself about it, take a deep breath, and just get on with it.

Here's what pruning can do:

-Contribute to plant health and thrifty growth. An overgrown shrub loses more than flowers, and unshaped trees look and are weak.

-Control growth. Keep plants away from wires and other hazards, exercise your choice of heights, decide how much and whether to prune crepe myrtles.

-Show off beauty with pruning to limb up a tree or shrub, cover an arbor, or maintain topiary

-Iincrease and enhance new growth, flowering and fruiting

-Prevent transplant shock

-Remove dead wood and hazardous or damaged trees

We prune because we are gardeners, because unlike so many things, the shears and saws are at our beck and call. When the plants respond well, you are cured of prunophobia.

Pruning Guidelines

To begin sorting out what to prune and when, think in terms of plant groups and their behavior.

cosmos

Annual flowers usually need old flowers removed (deadheading) and some types of annuals should be cut back at midseason. As annual flowers age, they form seed, ending the life of that plant to ensure the future of the species. When you interrupt this natural cycle by cutting the flowers off before they go to seed, the plants keep blooming. Happily, there are self-cleaning annuals that do not require deadheading. Begonias and impatiens are wildly popular in part because of this free-blooming habit. After a tough summer, these annuals respond well to rejuvenation. Cut them back in July to stimulate new growth, keep the plants neat, and bring on more flowers. If you want annuals to reseed, as cleome, Mexican hat, and Johnny jump ups do so readily, pull the mulch away from them as the flowers fade. Without good soil contact, most seed will not survive; if you don't want reseeding, keep the mulch pulled close.

Perennial flowers will not always rebloom, but deadheading them is still a good idea if you don't want them to reseed. Black eyed Susan, some coneflowers, and many daylilies do put on a second flush of flowers and they will look much better without the old stems and seedheads hanging around. Perennials with one primary bloom per stem, like daisies, have small, modified leaves below their flower. Cut their stems down to the true leaves and/or secondary flower buds. Once the stem is done, remove it entirely so others can emerge from the clump if they will. Others, like phlox, bloom atop fully leafed stems. Removing just the flower with a short stem will often stimulate blooms from other points on that stem.

56

When perennials are frost bitten, they often go dormant. A few are senescent, like Lenten rose and oxalis, growing from fall to spring and resting in summer. Remove the browned stems and rake away fallen leaves when this happens. If you don't, the weather is sure to warm up and get rainy. The result can be a nasty outbreak of furry fungus on the stems. Even if they don't hang around to infect future flowers, you'll inhale the spores when you finally do cut them down, and nobody needs more allergens

A huge issue for southern gardeners is that perennials do not always take a rest. Often lantana and verbena have already started to grow at their base by the time the mature stems finally turn brown. Butterfly bush is famous for staying somewhat green all winter, but still needs to be cut down to stimulate the new season's growth or it will become thickety with small flowers if any appear at all.

Ornamental grasses and clumping ground covers respond well to pruning annually to keep their clumps neat and bring on flowers. Ground covers like liriope look ratty when unkempt winter-damaged growth is not removed before new growth starts. Use a long-bladed hedge clipper to cut a few inches off ground covers and remove damaged leaves. Fountain grass and other large ornamental grasses develop an unattractive, sprawling habit unless cut down in winter. Cut the clump down to 12 inches to 18 inches tall, using a hedge shear held upside down to shape the grass into a rounded mass.

Bulbs, whether true bulbs like daffodil, or plants that act like them (rhizomes such as iris, tubers of canna, or gladiola corms) need little pruning, but we do it anyway. Spring bloomers use their green leaves to move nutrients into the bulbs, so the longer you can leave them be, the better. Once the leaves are half-browned, go ahead and cut them off if their appearance is unsightly. Likewise, it is fine to cut iris leaves into fans to improve air circulation in the bed as summer heats it up. Bulbs like caladium and dahlia that must be dug up in parts of the south and stored to ensure their survival will be best left to turn completely brown. Then trim off their foliage and proceed.

Roses. Here's the deal on roses. They fall into two main types, **hybrid teas** and **everything else.** If you don't know what kind yours are, look at how they're meant to grow. Hybrid teas have thick canes, usually with one cut-flower quality rose atop each stem. To get two rounds of these flowers, prune hybrid tea roses twice each year in mid February and late July. Cut the canes down to 18 inches tall in winter, two feet in summer.

The other roses grow like shrubs, with many stems and flowers on each plant. Usually they are lumped together and called shrub roses, old garden roses, antique roses, and other names. Some are all of those things! But they don't all need the same pruning.

Once-bloomers usually put on quite a show in spring, then grow grand green leaves and new canes all summer. Prune them after they bloom to shape and control growth. Remove the oldest canes entirely to ground level so new ones can thrive. Next year's roses will flower best on this year's strong new canes.

Climbers should be pruned like once-bloomers, but in fall. There are roses like 'Mermaid' that are huge and will continue to bloom without pruning. Unfortunately, these roses will also climb over your garage if you don't control them. Use jute to tie climbers to the front only of the structure. Avoid the temptation to weave the canes around pieces of jute or wire. In the fall, cut the jute and let the canes down on the ground. Prune for height and shape, and remove canes as they grow woody with age. I know this all sounds ominous, but do it once and the results the next year will stun you.

Low-growing, ground cover type roses are free-flowering and need be pruned only to remove dead wood and canes with strongly upright habit.

Vigorous reblooming (remontant) shrub roses will outgrow their space with weak growth and fewer flowers unless they are pruned hard in February. Cut off everything except the main canes and remove any of those that are weak or badly placed. Then cut the main canes down to about two feet tall. The idea is to push new growth to about the same height each year. When in doubt, prune these a bit more. With deadheading, they will flower several times beginning in spring. You can prune a few inches off in late July if necessary to neaten up the plants and spur on new growth and more flowers. This group includes the Texas found rose 'Caldwell Pink', 'Bourbons', 'David Austins', noisettes, standard size 'Meidiland' varieties, and many more. If February gets by you one year and the roses start to grow, leave them be and prune harder in summer.

A few types of individual roses hardly ever need pruning except to remove dead wood and old flowers so more can replace them. You can cut off some of their height in winter and in summer between bloom flushes. China roses ('Archduke Charles') and most of their relatives in the floribundas are in this group, as well as the butterfly rose.

Trees of all kinds need to be pruned while they are young to shape their growth and encourage sturdy trunks. Yes, they're small, but squint if you must and imagine them fully grown. Remove branches that crisscross the canopy or each other, and any weak wood, especially small branches low to the ground. Its important to take a look at trees each year, no matter their age, and prune for strength. In the case of single trunk trees with lots of side branches like Bradford

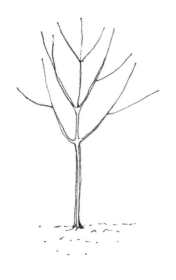

pear, limit the number of branches you allow to develop. Better air circulation around the major stems and less weight on them can work against their natural tendency to split in half in a strong storm.

Crepe myrtle is an example of a tree that responds to deadheading. It should be trained while young, and can be pruned heavily in winter. See page 86 for more explanation of crepe myrtle behavior and treatment in a special section on the South's favorite tree.

Flowering trees can be pruned after flowering has finished to shape the trees and encourage new growth.

Evergreen trees can be clipped and shaped in late winter, just as their new growth is beginning.

Shrubs may be the perfect plants to cure shear fear. Evergreens are the simplest to figure out, especially those that make berries or other winter fruit. After the birds have feasted in late winter, you can cut back mature evergreen shrubs by as much as one third their overall size in one year without harming them. Young evergreens will grow thicker if you will prune a few inches off in late winter and in early June for the first three years or so. After that, you can continue pruning, or not, as their appearance and your mood dictates.

If you must deal with overgrown shrubs, look before you bring in the chainsaws. You can limb up most of them, creating small trees. By pruning everything off the trunks up to a crown of a canopy, you gain a quality specimen that would cost a pretty penny to buy. Better yet, you honor that aging beauty.

When other considerations preclude limbing up, most evergreens can tolerate being cut back by as much as half. The result will be ugly, but with time and ample amounts of water and fertilizer, rejuvenation will work.

Flowering shrubs are pruned based on their growth habit and flowering time. Before you prune any of them, first think of when they bloom.

Spring blooming shrubs that bloom on one year old wood growing off the older wood will hold their flowers up in the shrub. Prune right after they bloom to thin the wimpiest of shoots on young shrubs, to remove twiggy old growth in older ones, and to remove errant shoots. Take a few inches off each branch annually to keep the plants healthy, properly sized, and flowering. This group includes forsythia, mock orange, weigela, and most of the spireas.

This summer's new growth will be next spring's old wood from which new leaves and flowers grow.

Flowering shrubs that bloom on one year old wood that grows right up from the base of the plant or near it can be pruned in one of two ways. Cut back to near ground level or to vigorous branches coming from the base of the plant such shrubs as kerria and abelia whenever they become twiggy or fail to bloom.

camellia

Camellia and azalea are the best examples of why we prune flowering shrubs within a month after they bloom. Winter and spring's showiest ladies begin to set buds for the next year almost immediately. If you prune later than a month after the flowers fade, you cut them off, and, no doubt, suffer a relapse of shear fear.

A few flowering shrubs bloom entirely on the **current year's wood,** such as chaste tree, Japanese beautyberry, St. John's wort, and butterfly bush. It is a challenge to prunophobics to cut these back as drastically as they need, but worth it when new growth bursts into flower.

Hydrangeas. Many kinds of hydrangeas have found their way into our hearts and gardens. Here is how to prune them.

> **Once-blooming Frenchies or mopheads** have been garden stalwarts for years, but our attitude toward them has changed. Where my grandmother cut them back hard each January, such drastic pruning is

60

not necessary or desirable except to rejuvenate very old shrubs. Instead, like the lacecaps, we prune French hydrangeas in winter to remove old flowers left on the shrubs. Clip the stem off behind the flower down to the next bud and remove any weak wood in winter. More often, once-blooming French and lacecap hydrangeas need only be pruned after they bloom to shape the shrubs and remove the oldest branches and those that are trailing on the ground.

Reblooming hydrangeas develop new flower buds on both last year's wood (old) and this year's new growth. Prune them only to deadhead the flowers and shape the shrubs during the growing season.

Oak leaf hydrangeas can be treated like mopheads and lacecaps. They do not have to be pruned at all, but can be to remove aging flowers and to keep new growth healthy. You can remove the oldest stems completely every few years so new ones will keep coming up. Do not prune any of the hydrangeas after midsummer, or you risk losing the flowers for next year. Prune as needed before that, even while the shrubs are in bloom if necessary.

Reblooming shrubs, such as Encore azalea and loropetalum, can be pruned after the first flush of flowers in the spring. Despite the rule about not cutting buds off, rebloomers will flower again in the same season if you prune them. Like 21st century hydrangeas, they bloom on old and new wood.

Tools for Pruning

Hand pruners. Every authority says to select a superior tool and keep it forever, but I am unable to resist a new kind of handle or blade material. Traditional clippers and pruners with their straight handles make you use repetitive motions and work you harder than is necessary! Once I moved to padded handles and ratcheting action to lower the impact on my wrists, I never looked back. Currently I use a ratcheting hand pruner for stems about half an inch in diameter, a straight line clipper with padded handles for smaller stems, and a long handled clipper that works by squeezing its handles together. This last enables me to reach nearly two feet to prune without stooping. Also in the greenhouse are serrated scissors, straight edge scissors, a pocket knife, and a grafting knife seldom used for its original purpose but excellent for cutting jute string.

Loppers and shears. A lopper has two curved blades set to slice through woody stems when brought together by the action of two handles. I use two sizes of loppers, one small, and two that are much larger. One of the larger loppers looks traditional with a blade that can cut a branch almost two inches in diameter. The other has a fantastic ratcheting head, allowing me to reach into or under a plant to prune it without contorting or overworking wrists and elbows. Hardly anyone uses grass shears any more, those spring action long skinny blades that cut crosswise. They are useful for cutting back grassy plants and keeping short borders neat. Their big brother, the two-handled, cross motion hedge shears, have no equal for shaping flowering shrubs, cutting back large grasses, and keeping evergreens neat. This is one tool I can maintain and so can you: the blades have a strong edge that is easy to sharpen with a small file.

Saws, short and long. Two saws compete in my garden for the title of Most Used, a nine-inch folding saw and a telescoping pole pruner that reaches 15 feet over my head. It is amazing what you can cut with such a small folding saw. Other saws are handy at times, as is an axe and a pick.

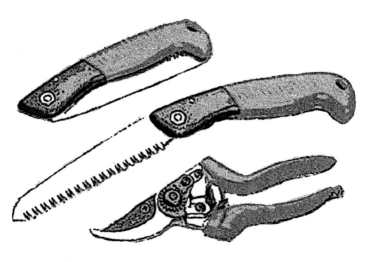

The efficiency of a small folding saw with large teeth is absolutely amazing! And a ratcheting hand pruner instead of a regular one gives you more power for the same effort.

Power to strength ratios. Though I use hand tools the vast majority of the time, my experience does include the big guns of the pruning world. When the branch to be pruned is too large or the job too extensive for hand tools to be practical, power tools amplify muscles nicely. Wear earplugs and safety goggles, please, whenever employing chainsaws and power hedge shears. And be aware of the decibel level you and your neighborhood can tolerate.

Hauling made easy. Carrying a tarp with you as you prune or groom plants just makes sense unless you have elves that come behind you to clean up. For big jobs, cut a large branch first and use it as a litter for everything else. Position the major piece of debris so its trunk or stem becomes your handle. Even with a tarp underneath, hauling is much easier.

Beans climb a bower made of leftover sticks.

Litter and leftovers. Should you grind, chop, compost, make wattles and bowers, or build forts? In our generous climate, there's lots of plant debris in even the smallest garden. It is fine to dig some of the lawn clippings and more of newly raked leaves into areas you intend to plant next year. Otherwise, compost what you can and throw away what you must. Don't miss an opportunity to use prunings for propagation, decoration, and construction of wattle fencing, bentwood trellises, garden bowers, or the eight-year-old's dream home, a fort made of hedge trimmings.

Know a pro. A licensed, bonded, insured arborist can be your best friend when grand old trees are yours to steward. Trees can hold up a hammock and shade your house, but they can also become hazards. Obviously, when damage to big old trees happens in a storm, professional attention is demanded. But other problems can evolve more subtly. You see the trees every day, and signs of distress can be overlooked. Besides being another set of eyes to watch for common problems as trees age, the arborist can tell you what not to worry about, and that may help you sleep at night.

A few professionals also provide deep root feeding; find one if you can. Alternatively, use an auger to fertilize by drilling holes around the drip line of the tree to put it where the tree's feeder roots can reach it.

Feel Shear Fear? Check Guidelines Here!

Change your attitude. Plants benefit from pruning and it is not hard to learn the basics.

Pruning is created by subtraction. It is more like sculpture than anything else, where the artist envisions the result and removes everything else.

See the line and cut to it. Look to find the growing point, the bud or node you want to be the top of the pruned plant, then cut backwards to leave it exposed.

You can always cut more, not less. Start at the outside of the plant, make the first few cuts, then step back, assess the result, and adjust before you continue.

Make slanting cuts. No matter what you're pruning, cut on a slant that slopes away from the inside of the plant. The idea here is to direct water away from the interior of the plant and train yourself to prune in a consistent manner.

Why Not to Paint Wounds

Old ideas die hard, including the use of black pruning paint on freshly cut surfaces. Some people still do it, thinking it will help the healing by keeping insects and pests out. In fact, painting seals in the anaerobic bacteria, those that need no oxygen to live in plant tissue and destroy it, leaving them free rein to do their damage.

Chapter 4. Pests or just Pesky?
How to Control Garden Raiders

As you cultivate to keep your bit of the earth in good health, a shift may occur in how you think about the creatures large and small that inhabit your bit of the world. From microscopic mites and a plethora of insects to voles and deer, there is a place in your backyard habitat for all of them. This goes even for the evil little squirrels, though I will continue to curse them when they hit me in the head with green crabapples!

I want to encourage you to increase the diversity of plants and avoid using pesticides randomly in your garden in order to improve the habitat for critters of every sort. Remember the four pillars of healthy habitat and provide places to nest and rest along with water and food resources. If you do these things, nature will take its course and you will have fewer bad bugs, because there will be balance in the habitat. Keep clippings and deadheaded flowers raked out of the beds, and mow the areas where it's tempting to let weeds take over. Remove those safe harbors for pests, take a brisk walk around the garden every day so nothing gets by you, and reduce or eliminate the use of pesticides, including the organic controls. Of course, there will be pests, but thrifty plants in gardens where beneficial insect populations can thrive will always be less vulnerable to serious damage from them. Take it on faith, or try it for a year and see for yourself.

The four pillars of healthy habitat: nest, rest, water, and food.

Beneficial Insects: Our Garden Angels

Not every critter, bug, or fungus will kill your plants. Think tolerance first. So long as they're not eating your plants, leave them alone. Some are simply a nuisance you can ignore or deal with, although it may mean putting up a fence against deer or rabbits. The garden angels, though, are your best friends because they feast on the bugs that eat your plants. Look for these beneficial insects and cultivate your microclimate to encourage them.

Ladybird beetles (aka ladybugs) have the advantage of being colorful and not at all threatening-looking. Spots dot their orange-red backs as they scurry around on your plants, merrily dining on aphids, scale insects (especially the crawlers, yum!), spider mites, and mealy bugs. This family of insects is huge, and most are helpful. But there are bad relatives. If you spot one with a bronzy color back (Mexican bean beetle) or three neat rows of black spots on a yellowish back (cucumber beetle), you're under attack.

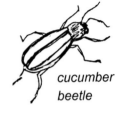
cucumber beetle

True bugs are a group you can watch work to know whether they're at work, beneficially. Larger than most of the pests, this posse romps quickly through the plants. They stick their victims and suck out their bodily fluids. Nasty to think about, but these very effective predators can only work if you let them alone. This may sound stupid, but before you pull out the pesticide, even the insecticidal soap, be sure the bug you see is actually eating a plant, not another insect. Watch for the well-named members of the predator posse:

-Assassin bugs have red bellies and seek out aphids and leafhoppers.

-Damsel bugs have long front legs that pinch their soft-bodied prey.

-Pirate bugs are painted in harlequin patterns, but are mostly beak, and are the nemesis of thrips.

Braconid wasps look like white spikes stuck to their prey, which includes tomato hornworms, aphids, and leaf rollers. Learn to love this sight, since it means you don't have to get out the BT to control many caterpillars.

Tachinid and syrphid flies are in the hoverfly group, so named because they fly like a helicopter. The T's are also called sweat bees and do mimic bees and wasps in appearance. They'll eat almost any-thing, including stinkbugs, thank good-ness. Syrphids look like little wasps, but let them be so their maggot babies can eat up the aphids in your garden.

praying mantis

Praying mantis, those angular green jewels, are not the most efficient of the predators, as they will eat aphids and unfortunately other predator insect larvae as well, but deserve to be left alone in most gardens.

Lacewings might be the most overlooked of the beneficial insects, and could be called the swans of the garden. The adults are lovely with mesh green wings dominating a tiny body. But the ugly duckling immature stage, the voracious lacewing larvae, are decidedly fierce looking, almost reptilian in demeanor. One's first instinct might be to squish the ugly things, yet you must resist. The lacewing larvae are called 'aphid lions' for good reason.

Spiders and toads are obviously not in-sects, but they benefit the garden greatly if you allow them to live in it. Daddy long-legs, jumping spiders, and many more eat any sort of insect they can catch. Toads are the slow and steady predators in your

Meet The Beetles

potato bug

If you meet the beetles, know that they are a lazy bunch. Get out to the plants early in the morning with a sheet. Spread it on the ground under them and shake the plants gently to knock the beetles off so you can get them out of the garden. Once they're up and awake, they're fast, and hard to spray or dust. This control method works for cucumber, Mexican bean, and Japanese beetles. In the long run, controlling the white grubs is the key to Japanese beetle control and may deter moles and armadillos, too. Treat the lawn with a product called milky spore, a disease that attacks only the grubs without endangering the other inhabitants of the soil.

---

garden. They keep their area clear of pests, so if you're lucky enough that one has burrowed into the garden, give him a name and thank him for his work.

Those Pesky Little Devils

Some critters are hard to tolerate. Consider the **rabbits, deer, armadillos, possums, voles and moles.** In cultivated areas of your property, a fence is the best way to exclude the first quartet of marauders. You can chase the rabbits out of the collard patch like my mother did, or hang up bars of soap to deter the deer, or spray daily to repel them. Don't give the armadillo or possum a way into the barn or greenhouse. They'll get a postbox and you'll never be rid of them. And don't overlook the importance of removing food and water sources. Pick up the food and water bowls each evening if you feed any animals outside.

When it comes to voles and moles, there are enough solutions to fill a dumpster, though few that are worth anything. Voles are little rodents a couple of inches long, mostly tail. If they have their druthers, they will burrow in the nice loose garden soil in your beds, eating plant roots until they can raise a family and eat the rest of your roots. Some gardeners will advise you to try and poison them, others say to tamp down the soil and/or increase or decrease the amount of

A rabbit family can eat you out of house and home!

mulch you use. The most effective vole control is having a cat who is allowed to hunt them. *Yes, I advise pitting the voles against a cat.* They will lose and the survivors will move next door.

Before the gentlest among you complains, I am acutely aware of the issues involving cats and gardens, but vole control is their forte. I do not have birdfeeders in my garden yet plenty of birds find it anyway, as do **squirrels, lizards** (superior gnat eaters, by the way), and occasionally, my neighbor's **pot-bellied pig.** We've established a certain rapprochement over the years and I encourage you to tolerate all the animals you can, too, in the name of ecodiversity and easier gardening. The squirrels keep to the oak trees that dot the property, while the birds nest in a thicket, in the shrubs and trees around the gardens edge. The

fungus gnat

Play Keepaway

Don't let bugs get to their banquet! In living with insects, exclusion is often the name of the game. Screen keeps the mosquitoes out of your porch, but draped over a hoop frame it protects young transplants from the cabbageworm moth and her associates. Woven fabrics lay over the entire row for the same purpose, and both do a fair job of keeping slugs and snails at bay. As you read about these and other devices I suggest using, do not imagine that you must have a garden entirely covered with plastic jugs, old screen doors stood up for shade, and screen boxes over every plant! I assure you they aren't all in use at once, and I do remove them when company is coming.

lizards hang out in the kitchen sink planted with aloe vera, dashing to the rooftop whenever the cats emerge from their sleepy stupor to patrol the courtyard. The felines make their way about the garden to sleep in the shade under a rosebush or tomato plant. It works for us.

Moles drive people crazy all out of proportion for the damage they do. I'm not downplaying the ruined lawn nor my father's serious attitude about them. However, the extreme lengths people go to often show little result, and that frustration is, I think, what deranges homeowners. Yet there are solutions. The raised runs created by moles are the key to disrupting them, along with controlling the grubs they seek in those tunnels they make. At the first sign of a run, stomp it down. When it reappears the next day, stomp it down again, or shove a garden hose into it and turn it on full blast. This is also the place to set the trap if you use one, but no, there are no live-catch traps for mole hunting. Metal rods with spinning whirligigs atop them are often stuck into the runs on the theory that their vibration upsets the moles. Might be, but the sight of a dozen or two of them in one yard isn't my idea of art. Control the grubs, stomp the runs, and worry about something important.

B.T. NOTE: Different little worms, actually moth (like hornworms) and butterfly larvae, plague many kinds of plants. But many are the future beauties you want in the garden, day and night. Try to tolerate minimal damage, physically removing the creepy crawlers you see from shrubs and perennials. If it becomes necessary to control the population more aggressively, use a product containing B.T. (*Bacillus thuriengiensis*), but be aware that it will attack all members of the Lepidoptera family, that is, all the butterflies and moths are susceptible to the natural predatory bacillus in B.T. or Dipel, another common name for this formula. It is another reminder that there are plenty of pest controls that come from natural sources and they are just as lethal as anything made in a lab. Their advantages begin with the fact that they work, but there are other reasons to seek out organic control products when pests persist and you've decided the plant must be saved. Organic and biologic controls are, for the most part and with notable exceptions, less persistent in the garden and therefore less likely to do in the next insect that comes along. Some also take longer to begin working but do a more effective job of controlling the population. For example, B.T. takes a week or more to get going, but once established will devastate the worms on the plant, and only on that plant. I advise plucking off every one you can see before spraying B.T. to infect the ones you can't see yet.

Bagworms and webworms. Some of the ugly pests and their bags and webs are best removed, even if it takes a bit of imagination to figure out how best to do it. Webworms and bagworms are clever rascals who spin a cover to protect their nest and sit happily inside. You can drench the tree in insecticide and it never touches them, but there are two strategies that usually work better. To whatever height you can reach, pluck off the bags. Use a broom wrapped in cheesecloth or something similar to collect the webs. For unreachable heights, use the strongest blast of water you can muster. There are hose attachments including long pipes to focus a blast strong enough to flake paint, and they knock the webs down, too. When the webs are breached the birds can work on the worms.

Real Demon Raiders

The real marauders in your garden are pests that work against your best efforts, and sometimes take advantage of your good intentions. Most plants can tolerate some pests for some time, and you shouldn't feel bad about the occasional ruined leaf. If you don't want to control insects, grow plants with bulletproof reputations.

Left uncontrolled for too long, each of these pests can kill the plants they inhabit. There are other pests, of course, with equally venal intent to particular plants, but the ones in this group are quite common to many plants. When you do have a plant under attack from insect or fungus pests, decide first if the plant is worth saving. If it is, use physical controls first, then target the plant with an organic pesticide that will control the problem, and treat only that plant if possible.

Piercing, Sucking Punks. This Group Drains Your Plants.

> **Aphids** have soft bodies about the size of a pinhead. They're round or pear-shaped, and come in different colors depending on their lifecycle stage and what they're eating. Aphids multiply every eight days and populations can build geometrically as they dehydrate the new growth of almost any available plant, often resulting in pale, dry looking leaves. Worse, plants can be stunted and even die.

> **Strategies:** Look closely at the aphids on your plant; if they are swollen and goldish colored, celebrate because natural predators are at work. Likewise, if you have aphids but also a large population of the beneficials, the natural balance may be enough to keep the damage at a minimum. Most plants can take a few aphids, and it's counterproductive to lose those feeding on them by using insecticides, whether organic or chemical formulas. If you see ants traveling about on your plants, control them because they farm the aphids, sheltering them from natural predators. To control both ants and aphids, first blast affected plants with strong streams of water daily. If the aphids are still

visible after two days of water torture, treat immediately and every eight days with insecticidal soap spray or spray or dust with a contact organic insecticide such as pyrethrin.

Whitefly is a winged insect a quarter to half an inch long. Its tiny young are non-airborne, white specks seen on leaves and stems, especially on the undersides. Seriously infested hibiscus, gardenias and other shrubs will yellow and their growth will stunt.

Strategies: Space new plants and prune established ones to provide good air circulation, and fertilize, but do not overuse nitrogen where whitefly is a problem. Remove plants that harbor whitefly such as littleleaf privet and golden euonymus. Their presence there may not be

an issue, but subsequent infestations on gardenia or crepe myrtle nearby can be. Young whiteflies can sometimes be dislodged with a blast of water, but usually they stick tight. This stage is not mobile, so insecticidal soap or pyrethrin sprays will control them. Since the adults fly away as you approach, spraying them directly is difficult. Sometimes they congregate on the plant at dusk, so a blast of water may drown some. Pyrethrin or Neem will have some residual effect while it is on the leaves. As a last resort and to save a particularly valuable tree or shrub, conventional advice would say to use systemic insecticides. However, there are no organic systemic insecticides. The systemic strategy that introduces the insecticide into the plant's system also puts every insect at risk of being poisoned. Especially indoors, some people have good luck with yellow sticky paper, which not only traps the bugs, but helps you monitor population buildups and guide your control efforts.

Leafhoppers can move both sideways and straight up. In addition, the adults can fly. Most often we see small multicolored wedges that jump right out of the way when disturbed. Young and adults dehydrate plants, particularly shrubs like azalea. When the population surges, leaves look mottled and may turn brown with curled edges

Strategies: Look for the signs of the first leafhoppers in early summer, shiny, brownish-orange dots of excrement. Annually, rake out the mulch under shrubs and replace it to destroy their nests. Introduce

green lacewings and practice good garden sanitation. Use oil sprays in winter and early spring. Treat at the first signs of damage with pyrethrin or neem sprays.

Scale insects look quite different on different hosts, but adults are lumpy shapes coated with waxy protective shells. You'll see various colored bumps on stems, bark, and/or leaves that look positively disgusting. Leaves on camellia, Japanese magnolia and other trees and shrubs can turn yellow and mottled when scale are feeding. In early spring, the crawler stage of scale hatches and searches for the perfect place to insert its beak and grow up. All stages cause twisted new growth, disfiguring the plant and sometimes killing it.

Strategies: Since adult scales are almost impervious to pesticide sprays and are too stuck to the plants to be blasted off with water, winter oil sprays are essential. When you identify the insect, usually in summer, scrape off all you can from large branches and prune out any small colonies on little branches and stems. Destroy all material you remove, then spray the plant with insecticidal soap to finish them off. Use oil spray in winter, then keep an eye out for the crawlers to hatch with the first new leaves on the plants. Spray them with neem at weekly intervals as long as you see new hatchlings.

White grubs, the larvae of June bugs and Japanese beetles, spend the winter under the lawn. Both kinds wake with the spring and feed their voracious appetites by eating grass roots on their way to emerging from the surface. Grass looks streaky and yellow, often in stressed areas or near concrete driveways, and has lost its roots. When it peels right off the soil surface, it's dead. Adult June bugs seldom do enough damage to plants to warrant control, but Japanese beetles adults can defoliate your rose garden in a day.

Strategies: Look for the adults and determine whether June bugs or Japanese beetles are present in the summer garden. Pick off the adults, or lay a sheet under the affected plants and shake the plants in early morning to knock the sleepers off where you can dispose of them easily. Treat the lawn with milky spore in fall and spring to begin  control, then annually in spring. This naturally occurring disease takes a year to be effective, but long term, it is the way to go. If June bugs are an issue, treat the lawn with parasitic nematodes. Japanese beetles are limited to one generation per year, fortunately, since they are capable of stripping an entire rose bush while you're away for the weekend. Their brief life happens in summer, and when they are sated, they mate and lay eggs in the soil. The grubs are shaped like the letter C and are the tasty morsels sought by the moles that tear up your lawn.

Chinch bugs are marked with a white crossways stripe on the back of their red or black, quarter-inch hard bodies. They take advantage of dry conditions in lawns to set up residence. The turf doesn't peel up as it does with white grubs, but does turn yellow first and then brown. The damage proceeds in an increasing circle; the appearance can be similar to lawns attacked by brown patch fungi, but its areas wax and wane with rainfall. To confirm the presence of chinch bug, cut both ends off of a coffee can or other similar cylinder and plunge it into the soil at the outer edge of the damage. Leave half of the can above ground and fill it with water to check for them. Chinch bugs will float to the top.

Strategies: Soak lawns at least occasionally to keep blades and thatch healthy. Fertilize annually and mow at the recommended height for your kind of grass. Specifically, mow your turf often enough to maintain the following heights without removing more than one third of the leaf blade in one mowing.

Bermuda 1-2 inches

Zoysia 1 1/2 to 2 inches

Centipede 2 to 2 1/2 inches

St. Augustine 2 to 4 inches

Note: Mow common Bermuda and common St. Augustine at the higher end of the range; keep improved varieties lower. Remove grassy weeds from your property because they can harbor chinch bugs, too. It's time to dethatch if the lawn feels spongy when you walk on it. This process is laborious and the lawn looks bad for a few weeks until it recovers. Use insecticidal soap sprays and, pyrethrin, or Neem to control chinch bug populations as soon as you find them.

Fungi Alert: Rusts and Molds

The list of pathogens that can attack plants is long and their life stories equally complex. My list is limited to the most common.

Sooty mold looks like its name. This flaky black coating covers all plant parts when it grows on them. Its preferred host is the sugary excrement of piercing and sucking insects, so it is found below them on the plant or on other surfaces under trees such as lawn furniture. It is most unattractive, and can make sitting spots sticky, ruin flowers, and, most seriously, interfere with basic plant growth.

Strategies: Remove sooty mold from plants with soapy water spray. In the case of concrete and furniture fabrics, scrub with manufacturers' recommended cleaning products. In the long run, however, prevent sooty mold by controlling the insects that provide its food, removing the conditions that favor its growth.

73

Rust, contrary to popular culture, does sleep. But the orange fungus waits for rainy, warm springs and then erupts, dotting iris and daylily leaves on their undersides. The dots soon turn into streaks, then entire leaves turn yellow and fall off to lie in wait in your mulch.

Strategies: Crowded plantings encourage rust outbreaks in many species. Dig and divide plantings at three-year intervals or whenever the leaves become so dense that you cannot see the ground. Clean up perennial beds every fall. Remove all fallen leaves and debris, work the old mulch into the ground and replace it. When rust appears, remove all infected leaves from the garden, and dust new growth with sulfur or spray with fungicide until fully emerged.

Root rot is caused by several pathogens usually present in our soils but can be imported with new plants or soils. Most woody plants can be susceptible, particularly holly and magnolia species. Flooding or constantly wet root zones exacerbate the issue for any plants that require good drainage to perform up to their potential. New shrubs can fail to grow and leaves may yellow all over the plant. Older plants infected with root rot wilt suddenly without dropping leaves.

Strategies: Understand the needs of the plants in your garden. Prepare new beds or planting sites to insure drainage adequate for that species. Avoid overwatering and dig a shallow ditch to divert floodwaters away when needed. If you suspect root rot and have altered the water profile around the plant, prune it by half. Drench the soil with a fungicide and spray new growth as it appears. Alternatively, dig up the plant, improve and treat the soil, then replant.

Organic Approaches and the Soil-Food Web

I learned to garden from my grandfather, the veteran train dispatcher known as Daddy Tom. His vegetable garden was two wide rows, each almost as long as the 100-foot fence behind it. He showed me how worms till the soil, and how to turn the compost and put in the eggshells and coffee grounds. He used barnyard fertilizers and nitrate of soda, lime and oak leaves to coax much of what our family ate out of the north Louisiana dirt. He taught me  to stomp and squish the worms on tomatoes and corn silks, and to pluck the lazy beetles off the beans. When the bugs got the better of something, he dusted with pyrethrin or sulfur if he didn't simply yank the offender out of the bed. Every autumn, he cleared the entire garden and planted alfalfa or ryegrass to dig into the soil in late winter. I clearly remember watching him one very wet day in February. He was standing in the muddy path between his rows, leaning his long frame over the raised bed to drop potatoes into neat holes. That winter was so wet we despaired of ever having recess again. If it wasn't actually raining, the school playground was a lake. Usually not allowed, we played jacks in the hall at school, and board games and jigsaw puzzles stayed on the table at home for days as we tried to amuse ourselves. Bored that day, I stood in the cold carport, put on my galoshes yet again, and went looking for Daddy Tom. When I found him, it registered with me that there was something different between the ground we stood on and that we gardened in, but it was years before I began to grasp the importance of that observation. He didn't call it organic gardening, he just did what he did and it was.

Only after studying horticulture in college did I realize just how much Tom knew about what to do, and when not to do anything. A perfect example of what he taught me is how important it is to take good care of the soil if you want it to keep growing. He and other adults talked in hushed tones about the Depression and the Dust Bowl, landmark events in their young adulthood that shaped their attitudes toward daily life. They stated frequently that if only everyone had known how to raise a few vegetables, some chickens, and a cow, much of the displacement and starvation of that era might have been avoided. I didn't make the mental connection then, but the soil-building methods he taught me kept his garden soil rich and our stomachs full. To see the difference, all you had to do is look at the soil he didn't improve. The utility area just off the garden wasn't abused, but could barely grow a green patch of weeds. I didn't know then what was going on in the soil, didn't know that my grandfather was nurturing the **soil food web.** That's what we now call the world of micro- and macro-scopic life that happens when roots meet soil. When it is healthy, roots can grow; when it's not, they struggle and so does the gardener.

Anyone who has ever turned a shovel of good soil has seen worms, rolypolies, bits of leaves, plain dirt, a few crunchy components, and maybe some stringy white stuff, among other life signs. In healthy soil you'll find up to 50 earthworms per square foot, but in that same space there are countless other soil organisms that are absolutely essential to its dynamic life. What you can't see are the microscopic residents, the invisible bacteria, fungi, protozoa, and nematodes, all fueled by carbon that comes from plant debris, soil amendments, and the life and death processes of other organisms. When you introduce a plant to the soil, its roots slough off natural secretions (carbohydrate exudates) as they grow. Ready and waiting are bacteria and fungi that live on root exudate, and the larger microscopics: nematodes (worms) and protozoa (think amoeba, flagellates, etc.). As is true throughout the animal world, the bigger creatures eat the

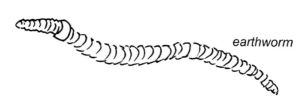

earthworm

smaller ones. In the case of the soil food web, what the nematodes and protozoa can't digest goes back into the soil to be absorbed as food by—wait for it—the roots! This marvelous arrangement goes on in what is called the **rhizosphere,** the busy hub of activity associated with plant roots in the soil-food web.

Not to be left out, the spiders, worms, and larger others that live in the soil eat the protozoa and nematodes. What they do not digest also stays in the soil and benefits its structure, adding to its gritty or smooth texture, and profoundly affecting its ability to drain excess moisture from the soil and hold onto it in dry times. The sticky bacteria and fungi adhere to the soil particles, holding them so roots can move into the spaces thus created. In clay and silt soils, the result is more porous soil, while sandy soils gain stability. The roots exude, the micro organisms are nourished, and then the macro organisms eat them. The roots absorb their leftovers, grow more, and keep exuding. These activities bind the soil particles together, and, thankfully for gardeners, result in more and better pathways through the soil for water and air. It is important to note that plants drive this whole business and reap its benefits since the superior soil environment spurs on better root growth.

We see the grand design of the soil-food web above ground, in plants with thrifty growth habits, plentiful flowers, and tasty edibles. But what of the pests? They are certainly part of the soil-food web, and from the gardener's point of view, here's where it gets exciting. Organic gardeners, including me, have asserted that they have less need for pesticides because beneficial insects and healthy plants aren't as vulnerable to the ravages of insects and diseases. It is not wishful thinking, it is true, and now I know why, thanks to researchers who search the soil with electron microscopes and study its every organism.

This is a daunting task, indeed, given that an average teaspoon of soil can have more than 20,000 species living in it. Not all of them are good blokes, of course, and some are nasty. If there are enough happy bacteria and fungi living in harmony with the plant roots, they don't want to be invaded and can often outcompete the invaders for the exudate both seek. Bacterial slime and fungi trap and exclude some pathogens, and they work together to form nets and sheaths that keep out others. A very special group of fungi, the **mycorrhizae,** bridge the barrier between animals and plants, forming a symbiotic relationship with roots. They gain root exudate to live on, then return the favor to act as physical protection and a fueling system for the roots in a most clever and mutually beneficial relationship. The good ambassadors of the soil food web limit the population of the bad guys in blatant self-interest, and I thank them.

The soil food web depends on the balance between huge populations of its members to survive and so sustain your plants. When the number of organisms is greatly reduced, the web cannot work, and the plants suffer. The truth is out: chemical fertilizers are salts, and while I have poured a bit of table salt into the stem of an invasive plant, it is not good for much else in the garden. The salts make the fertilizer components soluble, and they go right into the soil along with

the nutritive elements. Salt dehydrates bacteria and fungi as surely as it would a slug. When used regularly and exclusively, salts destroy whole segments of the microbial life underground. Once the four horsemen of decomposition are gone, the gardener must keep replacing the nutrients they would make if allowed, and the salts applied destroy more nutrients. The need for fertilizer increases when it could actually decrease in mature plants if they were nurtured in part by the soil food web. Part of the reason that organic gardeners say their garden is easier to maintain is because they have set up garden conditions that will ultimately let Nature take its course. You can fertilize less, not more, when you use organic fertilizers, nurture the web, and let it work without chemical bombardment.

Great numbers of microorganisms are needed to form the relationships that protect plant roots from pathogens in the soil. If you wipe out the good guys, leaving the root zone to depend on chemical fertilizers to stimulate root growth, the bad guys have a much easier time taking over, because their natural predators are diminished. The plants develop negative symptoms, and you use another chemical to try and fix that problem. It may work for the short haul, but the destruction of the root's protective layer by chemical fertilizers leaves it vulnerable to the next opportunistic pathogen that comes along. Organic fertilizers do not have this effect.

If you're going down this road, consider this information your crossroads and think about it. If your path includes regular use of chemical fertilizers, and you like the results, please nourish the soil food web twice a year in spring and summer. At least, top dress every growing surface in your garden with half an inch of compost annually in spring and work it in.

When we nurture the soil food web, we move closer to the natural balance our soil once had, before the land was leveled, before the house was built and the driveway poured, before chemical fertilizers and pesticides, foot traffic and other compaction brought on by us humans. Few of us can return our property to pristine, natural conditions, but we can take steps in that direction to huge benefit. Think about the needs of the soil food web as you choose products to use in your garden and you'll move towards organic and sustainable.

Healthy Differences: Diversity in Your Garden

It doesn't matter whether your garden is large or small, nor whether you grow in a garden bed or big pots on the deck: cultivate a broad range of flower types. When you combine plants of various heights, colors, and flower shapes, the result reverberates with beauty. Add organic gardening strategies to the diverse collection of plants and the whole thing hums with life.

Even if you like a bed full of one color petunia, the plants that surround it offer contrast. Often it is a dark green ring of monkey grass that frames the annuals inside. But when you plant different colors and heights in that same bed, they set each other off in natural synergistic beauty. Each looks better in context with contrasting and complementing companions. Further, you gain an extended season of flowering with different plants in the same color, carrying your theme through the year. Wildlife wins, from hummingbirds at eye level to pollinators and beneficial insects more likely to land on flowers blooming knee high and around your ankles. Bad boy insects find you anyway, so encourage the good guys by making the nectar they need easy for them to find.

Take this attitude of diversity a step farther and let a thicket develop behind the shrubs to offer shelter to the doves and toads, and any other backyard denizen seeking shade or rain cover. Offer water, whether a birdbath, a mister, or just a sprinkler going on a dry day. And yes, put up a bird feeding station for seed eaters unless you have cats.

Definitions

Organic means a product derives from nature. In terms of its impact on growing conditions, organic fertilizer is the mother's milk of garden soil. Pesticides of organic origin, on the other hand, are as toxic as their counterparts created by man.

Chemical means a product was created in a laboratory. It may or may not have a direct counterpart in the organic world. Chemical fertilizers disrupt the natural biology of garden soil; organic fertilizers do not. Even when other chemical products have the same working formula as organic products, their impact on soil may be very different because of their inorganic origins.

The Inevitable Caveats

We know that using pesticides indiscriminately greatly reduces the number of beneficial insects and predators in the garden. Yet there are serious pests that cannot, as yet, be controlled by organic means. Sometimes deciding what to control is simple. When a pine tree gets borers, it is tempting to try and save it with pesticide injections and sprays. But the tree will die anyway, as will many other insects in the wake of such treatments. Cut it down, plant something else, and spare the beneficials.

Other insects cannot be removed from the environment, yet they damage it daily and threaten vulnerable people. Imported red fire ants may soon have a natural nemesis, but until then, the targeted use of a fast-acting insecticide on the mounds makes sense. As their range increases with warmer winters, more gardeners will have to deal with them, and until a workable organic product is available, do what you must to protect yourself, small children, and pets.

Mosquitoes that carry West Nile virus must be avoided every day, all year round. Try repellants until you find one you can wear every time you go into the garden, even if it is not organic. The same goes for sunscreen and hats. I could tell you nightmarish stories about two dear people I know, but here is the short version. One didn't know what was wrong for weeks until the virus was diagnosed and had already taken a serious toll. The other celebrates each year of remission from skin cancer. Let that sink in, and hope you never hear such a story firsthand.

Integrated Pest Management

Each strategy to control the inevitable pests in your garden outlined in this book is based on the principles of IPM. This approach considers the big picture, the garden's overall ecology, while offering a path to follow that helps to keep it in balance. To practice integrated pest management, keep these principles in mind:

Choose varieties with known tolerance for common insects and diseases.

Set up traps in the garden, both to capture insects and let you monitor their population whether good or ill.

Observe your plants daily, or walk the garden every day.

Look for changes in growth pattern, egg masses, or chewed leaves, but don't miss the first flowers and honeybees, either.

Identify insects, mites, and symptoms of disease; do your research.

Determine the extent of the damage and monitor it, but also note the actions of predatory insects and limits of your distress.

Don't overreact. Physically remove insect pests with your hands or a strong stream of water. Rake up fallen diseased leaves and do not compost.

Cut down weeds near stressed plants and attend to their needs for water and fertilizer.

Proceed with caution, aware of the impact on the entire garden, not just one plant. Ramp up to controls that are organic when necessary to save plants from being overcome by pests, if the plants are valuable to you and if the controls have a reputation for working.

Know when to say when, and remove plants that cannot be grown without extensive pesticide intervention.

Above, a prized collection of cereus plants. Right, one of the lizards watchfully protecting the plants from pests.

Chapter 5. Two Plants and How They Grow

By far the most popular plants grown in the South are crepe myrtle trees and tomato plants and we take great pride in them. If there's room for either one, we'll try growing it. I'll discuss these two in depth because we grow so many of both, and because between the two we find most of the challenges we face in gardening generally. Whether you realize it or not, that basket of tomatoes you pick means you know about several important gardening practices that inform the way you grow many other herbaceous plants:

smart variety choices

soil preparation for good drainage

water and fertility management

trellising

insect control (aphids, hornworms)

and if you have lost a tomato to blight, you've probably learned a bit about insect vectoring and the value of mulch to prevent soil borne diseases from washing up onto the plants.

Crepe myrtles teach a few tricks of their own that translate into better care of other woody plants:

improved varieties for disease resistance, height and color choices

pruning to control growth and stimulate repeat blooming

insect-fungus relationships (whitefly-sooty mold)

propagation of woody plants

Take what I can tell you about these two Southern favorites and use it to grow them and a healthy gardenful of other plants.

Tomatoes

More than any other edible, we grow tomatoes. They're not the easiest vegetable to grow, and they are widely available from local farms in season,

and yet we persist. Why? Red fruit on the vine or a plate full of slices on the picnic table conjures up sun-soaked memories of summer. As children we may not have even liked to eat them, but tomatoes are as much a part of our inner summer movies as running through sprinklers, biking to the park, and eating snowballs.

As much as any other edible, tomatoes illustrate the changes coming to us via the new U. S. Department of Agriculture zone definitions, which are related to the change in weather patterns. Planting dates can be weeks earlier, and should be, since the end of the bearing season comes sooner, too. It used to be that only serious, competition quality growers set out tomatoes in March, even in Zone 9, because of the chance of late freezes. Nowadays, when the temperatures dip below 40 degrees at night, a layer of plastic acts like a hot cap or mini greenhouse to give us an early start. Most years in the last decade, tomatoes planted this way on March 15 in Zone 8 have done very well and only needed protection for a few nights. Since tomatoes set few fruit when night temperatures are above 70 degrees F, and those nights now begin in June, we are playing beat the clock. If we wait until April, or after the customary blackberry winter late freeze, to plant tomatoes, there's only eight or ten weeks to grow before fruiting stops. Some may caution that if stunted, tomatoes won't grow, and that is true, but those who love their 'maters will just replant and talk for years about that freaky spring when cold weather got them.

Top Tips for Growing Amazing Tomatoes:

Soil to grow tomatoes must be well-drained so it can handle the huge amounts of water and fertilizer you'll need for maximum success. I would venture to say soil difficulties, whether density or blight pathogen populations, move more people to grow tomatoes in containers than any other consideration. Soil amended as described in this book grows fine tomatoes, and so does the potting soil recipe. A friend once remarked that a landmark in her life rearing two athlete sons was the day a twenty dollar bill no longer fed the growing teenagers at a family-style cafeteria. That made me think of tomato plants as the teenagers of the vegetable garden, always ready to eat and able to drain a gallon of milk overnight.

In a well-drained soil, with no rain, tomatoes need water every day. Get a rain gauge or poke your finger into the soil, but know if the soil is drying out excessively between waterings. Don't wait for the plants to wilt! Soaker hoses are best for vegetable beds, anyway, and the average one will do the job in about half an hour, depending of course on the water pressure in your neighborhood. Use your favorite fertilizer as often as the label describes, or slightly more often as a slightly lower rate. As soon as you plant tomatoes, put up the tomato cages or stakes. Not only will the plants grow faster than you might imagine, the cages make perfect frames for grow cloth to exclude insects from small plants, or to add a plastic wrap on a cold night.

Mulch. Tomatoes are one of the few plants that beg the question of mulch. General garden advice generally ends with the exhortation to water in and mulch no matter what the plant. A layer of organic mulch in late spring and summer helps to keep the roots cool, which is just what you don't want early in a tomato plant's life. Black plastic mulch certainly warms the soil, but may keep the roots too hot in summer. If you use it, plan to remove most of it or add pine straw or ground bark when daytime temperatures stay above 80 degrees to reflect some of the heat. Tomato plants are pest barometers at times, subject to nearly every sort of attack possible. Included elsewhere are aphids and whiteflies. Their diet surely includes tomatoes, especially early in the season when their other favorite hosts aren't quite as green.

Hornworm is a serious pest that can strip a tomato plant clean in no time flat. The green, inch-long larvae are well camouflaged on the stems, so the first 'sign' you may see is black pellets on the leaf surface. They grow in a few days to five inches long and as big around as your little finger, boasting bold black stripes and a fierce horn on one end. Not only tomatoes, but peppers and eggplants can host hornworms. Big brown moths lay the eggs that become hornworms. Exclude them with floating row cover if the pests have been a problem in previous seasons. Rotate tomato plantings each time you plant. Watch for young hornworms and their excrement and remove them from the plants with fingertips or tweezers. Or employ tweenagers (the new demographic of 9 to 12 year olds) to go on a search and destroy mission in the live video game outdoors, collecting hornworms for valuable prizes. Usually by the time you apply a pesticide dust, the damage is done.

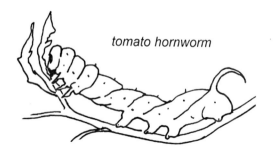

tomato hornworm

Stinkbugs Good and Bad. Less than an inch long and shaped like a shield, stinkbugs are so named because they smell bad when you squish them, but the damage they do to your ripening tomatoes stinks worse.

Careful, though, since these baddies are sometimes accompanied by a chaperone, the good stink bug whose only mission is to rid the world of the others. Most often you'll see only the ones poking about in your fruit. The adults linger over winter in the weeds along the fence, in a ditchbank or another unattended area. They get busy when daytime temperatures reach 70 degrees, laying eggs on a variety of vegetable and ornamental plants. Unfortunately, the whole family (from babies through every nymph stage) sits down for a family reunion style feed, poking their noses into the fruit to suck out its precious liquids. At the same time, as if the feeding wasn't enough, stinkbugs inject toxins into the fruit's skin that interfere with ripening. The tomatoes turn colors unevenly and may have yellow areas that never redden. You wait and wait, then finally cut into one to find that the fruit has gone way past pulp. Mama lays the barrel-shaped eggs in May or June and nymphs hatch ten days or so later. Watch for the adults early and the nymphs that follow. Stinkbugs are often the insects that finally take out the spring tomato plants because they are difficult to control without harming beneficial insects. If you have harvested the majority of the tomatoes by the time the stinkbugs get a grip, rip the plants up and remove all their debris from the garden, including any mulch that could be a hiding place for the next generations. Rotate the tomatoes to another place in the garden for the fall crop, too.

V & F wilts, very bad or fatal. Two fungus diseases display almost the same symptoms and preventing both is best done by choosing varieties that resist them. V is for verticillium wilt, F is for fusarium, or you can use my designations. V is for Very bad, F is for Fatal, because that's their results. There is no chemical control for either. V happens in cooler weather, earlier in the season, and can be aggravated by overwatering. Lower, older leaves wilt, yellow, dry up and die. The disease moves up the plant, yellowing the center leaves first. If fruit forms it is small in size and bland in taste. F wilt favors warmer weather, and affected lower leaves wilt and turn brown before the disease kills the plant. Since early planting can mean the soil is still on the cool side, mulching tomatoes early is not recommended in order to allow sunlight to warm the soil. Yet mulching could help prevent these soil borne organisms from splashing up and infecting your tomatoes.

Early blight fungus shows up first as leaf spots, distinguished by a yellow outer ring around a brown center. It worsens in wet years but is always around as heat and humidity build up in late spring. These bullseyes soon link up to brown the leaves and kill them, all over the plant. When the leaves drop, the fruit loses its natural shade and may develop scalded spot and sunburn. If the fruit are infected, the stem and top of the fruit can blacken and rot. If this disease appears on young plants before flowering, consider replacing them and planting in another part of the garden. But when it occurs after fruit is on the vine, try to stop it so you can harvest at least some of the tomatoes. At the first sign of the bullseye spots (another reason to walk the garden daily—these things spread fast) begin spraying the plants with a fungicide and continue weekly.

Spotted wilt virus. Leaves curl up and look chlorotic, and broad dark areas form at the stem end. Growing tips curl up, too, and the whole business wilts. Spotted wilt gets to your plants not from the soil, like the fungus diseases, but from an invasion of thrips. These tiny insects used to be tropical, but no more, and as they have spread, so has this virus. Thrips are tiny and lay their eggs in petals (like roses) or leaf tips. If you can see them—get out your magnifying hand lens—a high pressure water spray may help roust them, or a very localized spray with pyrethrin or neem. The virus spreads quickly from their feet to the plant, making control very difficult. Ongoing garden sanitation is the best preventative of thrips, and so spotted wilt virus. Rogue out young plants with this virus, spray older ones for thrips if practical to hold down its spread, and space spring tomatoes further apart than the fall crop for better air circulation.

Leaf curl without spotting is a physical problem, not a disease, which is caused when wet soils get wetter. When conditions improve, the leaf uncurls. Other physiological disorders include cracks and catfacing, both related to fruit development and not treatable once apparent. The most common of these disorders is blossom end rot and the information about moderating water to avoid it should help with the other potential problems.

Blossom end rot, aka The Heartbreaker. Right at the time when the tomatoes should be filling out, the bottom (where the flower used to be) turns brown and blackens. To prevent this disaster, tattoo this on your head: monitor tomato watering practices carefully from the time you plant until you rip the plants out at the end of the season. In a nutshell, the heartbreaker happens when cells collapse because they couldn't get enough calcium at some point along the way. That happens because water was not consistently available as the plants grew, especially too much one day and too little the next. If your tomato plants wilt between waterings, you are stressing them and setting up the conditions for this fruit disorder. Calcium and Epsom salt sprays may help, but you don't need them to prevent blossom end rot.

Suckers. As the plants grow, the main stem goes up and the branches go out from it. When another stem pops out of the space between those two, it's called a sucker. Whether to remove them or not is a poser, if you ever even notice them. My grandfather insisted that his tomatoes would have no suckers, believing they would sap the strength the plants needed to ripen fruit. Other gardeners say to leave them for the added shade they offer to the fruit. They will root easily, so I use them as cuttings to start new plants for the late summer/fall crop.

Predators. You've heard of kids who pick plums or pears too early, take a bite and throw them down. They're predators as surely as the squirrels and birds who pluck a tomato, poke into it, and leave on the ground for you to find later. Sometimes they wait for it to be ripe, other times they go for the green. Deer leave less evidence, other than hoof prints, but will eat the succulent, fully ripe fruit. Fences and netting make the most difference, but if water is available elsewhere in the garden it can help keep them away. Soaker hoses and sprinklers, birdbaths and misters, a shallow pan of water—any of these might do the trick. The children have parents you can call, but unfortunately, the other tomato predators do not.

Harvest Notes. The idea of picking vine-ripened tomatoes has universal appeal, but may not be the smartest strategy. Hold pests and predators at bay by picking fruit as soon as it is pink at its shoulders, the widest point on the fruit. Let the ripening proceed safely indoors or in the potting shed, wherever indirect light can get to them and temperatures are mild. Never refrigerate fresh tomatoes, or risk a decidedly less tasty experience.

Crepe Myrtles

Crepe (often spelled crape) myrtles are much abused, yet usually bloom anyway. Lesser trees would die, but crepe myrtle endures improper planting, rampant watersprouting, insect attacks, and sooty mold with equal aplomb. Steel Magnolia, my foot! Crepe myrtle is the tree that represents the strength and tenacity I can identify with, so perhaps the phrase should be 'Iron Myrtle.'

The Right Crepe for the Right Place

Just because crepe myrtle will grow anywhere doesn't mean she should. Back when the choices were limited to tall varieties, we weren't deterred, because we wanted the papery flowers. Thousands planted crepes near the house eaves and under utility wires. When they grew too tall, gardeners learned to limit their height with severe winter pruning, lately known as crepe murder. Now crepes come in sizes from ground cover to head high, including weeping varieties, and stunning specimens that reach 25 feet tall in a few years. If you want to plant a crepe myrtle these days, or if someone suggests one for your landscape, ask its name and size at maturity if you want to enjoy its company without the chore of major annual pruning.

What to Do. Many people buy a house and the crepe myrtle blooms lushly in summer. The leaves turn a bright yellow or red as winter approaches, then drop and reveal the fine bark at its beautiful best. Shortly after the New Year, the homeowner notices all the neighbors and their landscapers armed with big saws, crepe myrtle squarely in their sights. They remove all the branches that sprouted last year and cut the trunks right off about eye level. The trees recover nicely and bloom like a lollipop in front of every house on the street. In the name of neighborhood harmony, I'd keep pruning those the same way your neighbors do, but if you want to stop chopping other myrtles in your yard, you can.

In January, look where the crepe has been repeatedly pruned and you'll find a knob, or a growing point, where the new sprouts emerge. Select one or two of those sprouts to cultivate and remove the rest. Suppress any other sprouts by clipping them off whenever they appear the first year. The one you left will thicken over time, the tree will grow taller and resume more of its natural upright vase form, and yes, it will bloom.

Excessive pruning sometimes causes lots of small shoots to spring from the base of the crepe myrtle trunk. When the trees are planted with lawn grass growing right up to their trunks, the fertilizer for the turf can be absorbed by the tree. More sprouts are stimulated by the excess nitrogen in the lawn food! Worse yet, you have to use the lawn mower or string trimmer to cut the grass right up to the trunk. One bad pass cuts the trunk, opening it to insects and disease. Clear the area around the base of any tree you plant in the lawn. Create a mulch circle or a flowerbed beneath it to prevent damage and lower maintenance time.

This calendar is designed for growing young trees into large floriferous ones and to maintain the Iron Myrtles you already have.

If crepe myrtles are planted in plenty of sun, but still don't bloom, prune each branch back by a few inches in summer, or cut back each branch by half its length in January. As a last resort, try to stimulate the trees auxins (they control these things) by whipping it. Yes, take a sturdy watersprout or other switch and slap

CALENDAR OF CREPE MYRTLE CARE

Jan-Feb   *Prune hard if you must, or simply cut off errant sprouts and twigs; replace mulch.*

Mar   *Apply fertilizer when new growth sprouts (unless you fear a late freeze!).*

April   *Watch for water sprouts and remove them while very small.*

May   *Celebrate first flowers; prune to train young trees; water regularly in dry springs.*

June   *Apply fertilizer whether you have done so already or not.*

July   *Deadhead flowers and water weekly, deeply. Control insects. Prune to shape.*

August   *Deadhead flowers and water weekly, deeply. Control insects. Prune to shape.*

September   *Deadhead flowers and water weekly, deeply. Control insects. Prune to shape.*

October   *Enjoy fall color.*

November   *Apply fertilizer without nitrogen to strengthen young trunks; plant new trees now through February.*

December   *Admire winter form.*

the trunk a dozen times. It may help, it may not, but this folk remedy won't hurt and surprisingly, some trees respond. You have my permission to do this at night so the neighbors don't get worried about your sanity. If it works, you can tell them why.

~~~

I wouldn't know how to garden without growing tomatoes, and I do like crepe myrtles, especially the varieties with peeling bark, so attractive on a winter day. No matter how serious I am about growing plants, it's their innate beauty and attractive arrangement in the garden that keeps me out there day after day. It's also the biggest challenge of maintaining a garden over time, and worth a special chapter in this book.

Chapter 6. Garden Planning, Garden Planting

To begin a garden or keep one going, make a mental picture of what you want the place to look like. Add to that the time you have each week to devote to transforming that vision into reality and divide by your budget. A reality check is often necessary to keep garden plans grounded.

This is a gardening book, not a landscaping book, but looks are important when selecting and placing plants. A happy, healthy plant is always more attractive than one that is struggling, but since that is only one part of the picture I offer some easy and practical pointers on design. You'll be thinking about how to make your outdoor living areas look nice and coordinate with the style of your home. You want to decide how to allocate outdoor space for your favorite activities, and how to improve the views from your windows so that you look out on beautiful garden scenes that express your personality.

I'll readily admit that my own quest for a beautifully laid out garden has seen its fits and starts. But I've picked up a tip or ten from some of the best and here's what I've learned:

You need a plan, but it's the rare soul that starts with a blank slate and an unlimited budget for architects to put the dream on paper. Even with those luxuries, the smart gardener makes a simple plan and prioritizes the garden's development. Gather these supplies: graph paper, notepad, colored paper (sticky notes if possible), pencil, ruler, measuring tape, camera, and, if possible, a friend. Now measure the real property, which is much easier if you have someone to help hold the tape and walk off the perimeter and general distances to the house, etc. I promise you won't remember even the most regular measures in the right order if you don't write them down as you go.

Step back once this is done and start taking pictures of the property in broad views to record everything that is permanent including structures, outdoor cooking/entertaining areas, existing trees and garden beds, utilities, paths, walls, dog runs and playground equipment. Sit down and transfer the measurements of reality to the graph. Honest, this is easier than you remember from school. Say the front of the property is 100 feet and it extends 80 feet deep, a great fit for a standard size piece of paper. Take a sheet of graph paper and fold it in half, then in half again. Unfold it. If your property is not rectangular, trim the paper or shade out the area that does not conform. Use the ruler to draw a ten inch line on the long side of the graph paper. That represents 100 feet, which means each inch is ten feet.

Figure out what is in the center of the property and sketch its shape at the center of the unfolded graph paper. Refer to the pictures and measurements you took and sketch in the features of each quadrant using the one inch equals ten feet rule. After the rough drawing is done, you can graph each quadrant on its own entire sheet of paper for a larger view. Yes, you can do these things on the computer, or get a teenager to take it on as a project.

Next, take a sheet of paper and fold it in thirds. On the first third, note what you want right away in your garden. The list might include a grilling area, a rose bed, a kitchen garden, a tool shed, but it's what you want first. List the longer range improvements you want to make soon on the second tier, and the 'wouldn't it be nice' list on the third. The last could be a lap pool, for instance. Knowing what you want eventually informs what you do now. If the lap pool is on your wish list, leave a sunny strip of lawn now and there'll be less to undo later. Tap into your inner kid and cut out simple shapes to represent each addition you want to make: red for the immediate needs, blue for the 'soons', and green for the 'much later' list. Start putting the shapes on your graph paper, and rearrange until you are satisfied. Reality will intrude as it did when my son wanted a pitcher's mound where my perennial border fit nicely in the plan. I moved it to the 'later' list, and when he went to college, the border began. Do make your plan, but keep it flexible.

Your garden is put together from elements that can match, harmonize, or contrast with each other. Each creates a different effect, sets the tone, and interprets your mood depending on how you use its lines, forms, and colors to sing your song.

First things first. At the top of your list should be drainage issues, with plans for grading and slope work if necessary to keep water away from structures. Watch the property on a rainy day to see where it goes, and where it stays. If the lawn puddles, or one bed never drains, deal with it on the front end of this project. The solutions may be as simple as elevating the lawn's dip with sand, or as complicated as swales or French drains. Get rid of obvious hazards right away, such as dead trees near structures or looming over your new border.

Things to Think About as You Plan:

Style and materials express harmony, or discord. Work with what you've got. If the house is formal, go with the symmetry of neat rectangular beds, at least in the front garden. If the house could be described as rustic, think open and casual and featuring native plants. The clean lines of modern architecture deserve to be surrounded by forms that soften them and anchor their shape to the earth without cluttering their good looks. When it comes to choosing materials for garden hardscape, it's more important that they match or harmonize with one another than which material you choose. For example, the finest wrought iron patio furniture looks out of place under the beams of a wooden arbor, but appears in perfect proportion to a wire sculpture arbor of similar size.

Focal points are special. Cast your mind back to the prettiest garden you ever visited and focus on what you remember. I'll wager there was a lovely plant grouping with a trellis at its center just off the porch, or a stunning statue at the end of slate patio, or a path where each curve revealed another vignette that burned into your brain. These are focal points!

When you glance out the window and right away, your eye is drawn the birds at the feeding station located just outside, you have found another focal point. It grabs your eye because of its prominent placement as well as its attractive qualities. One big shade tree in the front lawn is a focal point, but two big trees flanking the entrance aren't. Instead, they frame and call attention to the front door, which becomes the entry's focal point.

To find the logical places for eye-catching views outside, start inside your house and look out the windows that face the garden. Stand at the door and see what frame falls into your line of sight. Go upstairs and out on the porch to check the view from there, too. Take pictures if you want, or have that helpful friend stand in the yard and move at your direction to locate the best spot, the place you want to highlight, the focal point. Now go out into the yard and repeat the process from several vantage points. Some focal points are at the center of a small garden niche and must be explored to be experienced. But others, such as large pergolas and shade trees, deserve to be located so they are immediately appreciated from several directions.

The view from your back window may include a wide expanse of lawn highlighted by a tree at the back fence, and if it satisfies your eye, your search for a focal point is done. If it doesn't, pick a spot closer to the window and envision something there - another tree, a seating area, a pond, a birdbath. Your attention will be drawn to the nearer view, and you can enjoy it without squinting. No matter what size the space is, the mathematical magic is that a focal point in the

near view puts the far view into perspective. The depth of a space can be lost if the only lines and forms are at its perimeter. That's why a small garden looks larger when it has a winding path dotted with large plants or pedestal pots in its curves. It's also why large gardens are often divided by beds surrounded by lawn. The beds themselves become focal points, and stage your view from any distance. Your eye is led through them and the effect is more intimate despite the large space.

Borders and garden beds carry your message. You're a gardener and the spaces you create reflect your sense of the place. Two specific features, garden beds and garden borders, can be your best ally by giving you a destination to express yourself. In turn, they provide places to grow plants and focal points in the landscape. Here's the technical difference between the two: a garden bed is meant to be viewed from all angles, but a border has a definite back and front. It's not that beds are small and borders large, but rather where they are placed that matters. Every garden large or small should have a treasure, a small gem of a bed that comes into view as you turn a corner or round a tree. A border along the back fence featuring early spring-flowering shrubs will be a welcome surprise when everything between it and your house has dropped its leaves.

Repeat colors, plants, or themes in beds and borders for a unified effect throughout the garden. Repeat the colors of your house, echo or contrast them with the plants, and say what you want to say by repeating themes such as native plants or water gardens or night blooming flowers throughout the garden.

Edibles are beautiful, too. An excellent reason to go organic is the opportunity it offers to grow edible and ornamental plants together without the need to remember what pesticides you used where and when. Keep practical considerations in mind—you don't want tomatoes in the shade—but exercise some art, too. Put a persimmon tree in the front flower bed and let its orange fruit be a natural part of Halloween decorating. Grow a barrier hedge of blackberries and thorny shrub roses for beauty and sustenance. If you do give a particular area over to vegetables, herbs, and fruit, define it with the same materials you've used elsewhere to tie the kitchen garden in to the rest. Repeat picket fencing or a low wall, use the same edging, or paint the gate to match your front door.

92

Fencing, netting, and other distractions to keep everything from deer to bunnies out of your food are often necessary and belong in your plan. Food gardening at home is the hottest trend in gardening. For my money, a good fence around food growing areas is a better investment than a tiller. Remember, you only need to till or seriously dig into most of our native soils once, when you first make a garden bed, and you can rent the machinery for that at a daily rate.

Wildlife needs a place. In your initial look around the property, you no doubt made space for necessities, like utility access, cooking areas and kid spaces. I hope you also made room for what delights you, a hammock or glider and a collection of camellias, perhaps. Please put 'room for wildlife' on your high priority list, for both the two- and four-legged sorts. Children need a place to play outdoors that encourages their creative juices. Keep that concept in mind and use it as motivation to provide a thicket, a tent, a fort, or a wall with hay bales behind it. Yes, you may have to send them out there at first, but soon they'll leave the video game world for the wilder world you know and love. Simply by setting aside wild space, you provide a safe place for them, a nest if you will, and a resting space between games out on the lawn. Add a picnic basket and their needs are met.

Use the same criteria to create a garden where birds, butterflies, frogs, and natural predators can thrive. The four principles of backyard habitat are food, water, rest, and nest. Food comes in flower nectars, seeds, berries, and fruit provided by your plant choices. If a bird bath or other permanent water source is not possible, fill metal pie tins with water and place them in the sun, or run an arching sprinkler regularly and watch the fun. Rest means a hangout space, hidden from predators and hot sun, like a thicket, but it also means a flat rock for butter-flies to sun on. Nests are obviously birdhouses, but also include anywhere safe enough for your creatures to raise a family.

Be waterwise. We all have growing concerns about natural resources and weather patterns that give us too much water now and none later. Indeed, rain barrels and cisterns are back in the most sophisticated garden designs, along with drought tolerant plants. Make decisions on the front end about how you are going to apply and restrict water to your garden. Ditch around, direct towards, but figure out how to manage water. As you plan, make it a point to group plants with the same water needs together. Select the right plants for the natural water patterns in your garden if you don't plan to alter its terrain.

Practical gardens can be pretty and comfortable. The primary appeal of raised beds and gardening in containers lies in their simplicity, but they have considerable design strength as well. Raising the planted area gives it emphasis and makes it a center of attention, whether it is a perennial bed or a pedestal topped with a fancy pot. Elevating beds and borders by even a few inches above ground level improves their drainage, as does mixing your own potting soil for that container. Install higher sides of cinderblocks or wood frames and you gain access to your plantings without bending and stooping. Taking these practical steps for comfort and better growing can work as focal points, visual surprises, and add height to the scene.

Garden upward for inspiration. When the day has been tough, I sit in a chair under the tall trees and stare up. There's something about oak tree branches against the sky that never fails to lift my spirits. This fact is no epiphany on my part—water gardens traditionally have plants in them, on their surfaces, and at their margins pointing heavenward for the same reasons. As you plant and decorate the garden, don't be flat. Use trellises to increase growing space by going vertical and gain the upright effect even in very small spaces. After all, the great outdoors is a three dimensional space, so use it to inspire but also to unify your house with the earth below. Remember the house is the centerpiece of your garden at its largest view. Reinforce its lines by repeating them in the garden and both will deliver comfort and inspiration.

Less is often more. Whether you are enhancing an existing garden or starting a new one, establish some strong focal points and build around them. Give yourself more time than you can imagine you'll need to do projects large and small, and increase projected budgets by 10%. Garden projects are not supposed to be high pressure, so plan, be flexible, and stop and have some lemonade when it's going well, but also when it's not.

You may not be a landscape genius but every gardener can adopt, borrow or adapt the look of a nice vignette from anywhere and bring it home in spirit if not in exact species. Take pictures, ask questions, and don't be shy about getting what you like and avoiding what you don't, whether you do the work yourself or hire someone with landscaping expertise.

Planning and Planting Tips

Wet soil. Never walk on prepared soil, nor dig in wet soil. A great part of getting soil of any kind ready for planting is aeration. That's why even a wise no-till gardener will occasionally turn the soil, if only to incorporate green manure or other amendments. Remember that oxygen goes into the soil as water and its presence is crucial for healthy soil structure. You probably went to some effort to get the beds ready, and every step you take into the prepared soil compacts it horribly. All the air pockets get squeezed, the materials adhere to each other, and nothing relieves the impact. Except you, using a digging fork to work it up again.

I once lived where springs were notoriously rainy, so I decided to grow herbs and vegetables in raised beds. It was a lot of work at first building the frames and hauling the soil mix into the small urban garden. My neighbor watched the bed-building process that fall as she sat on her deck reading the Sunday newspaper. Come spring, I was harvesting lettuces when the neighbor decided to dig a garden plot in the backyard. She got a tiller and fought the soil until she had a couple of rows, and then the rains began. Frog-soakers, regularly, for weeks. I was able to plant and weed in between the thunderstorms, though I remember it as a fine year for aphids and mosquitoes, too. My neighbor trudged into her plot, its rows nearly level with the ground from the force of the storms. She carved out holes and planted tomatoes and peppers, squished back out and glared at me. I wasn't really staring, but it was quite a sight. I know because I was sitting on the back steps reading the Sunday paper at the time. Her plants were stunted, of course, along with her good intentions. That soil never dried out again and her footprints stayed smushed into the garden, a reminder of the truly fragile nature of wet soil. You can, in fact, do more harm than good.

Mulch first, then plant. When you're staring at a bare mattress, the first instinct is to put sheets on it. Same thing goes for naked garden beds. With mulch, many weeds never get a chance to land on the soil or push up through it, soil moisture is retained, and the whole business looks neater immediately. When you're planting a patch of annuals, particularly, it's much easier to part the mulch and use a trowel to pull back some soil than to plant and go back around with the mulch. Try it.

Use evergreens for stability. Remember that evergreens are, well, evergreen, and that they are usually quite long-lived. These realities should direct you to plant them so that you and everybody else can live happily ever after. The clever placing of evergreen sasanquas (*Camellia sasanqua*) at the back of a large border ensures that all eyes will be directed up to their flowers beginning in October. At that point in the year, most of the shrubs and perennials in front of the evergreens will be less interesting than at other times. But it is also possible to use

95

evergreens for evil, especially when planting them as screens. Those ligustrums and narrow cypresses will be large trees sooner than you think. Planted street side to block the view of cars passing a corner house, they can lend stability in the form of a perimeter, but are impossible for drivers on the street to see around and are dangerous for them to navigate around. Likewise, eleagnus makes a magnificent dense barrier, a solid silvery green form year round. But if you underestimate this plant, it can become The Blob that eats your space. Let elegant evergreens be the stalwarts that they deserve to be and give them the space they will demand, anyway.

Think seasons. As you gather plants for a new garden or if an established bed doesn't please you, think seasons. Granted, it's hard sometimes to adjust our seasons with the calendar, but we do have them. By putting a seasonal focal point in the garden that reflects your experience, you strengthen its sense of place and make it more interesting year round. The whole garden can reflect the seasons: a flowering cherry for late winter in the front yard, spring azaleas in front of the house, hydrangeas for summer around the back deck, and fall's beautyberry with its dazzling purple berries along the back fence. Add a holly hedge to show off its berries from fall through winter to complete the cycle. Or an individual bed can move its flowers and colors through the year: a crepe myrtle tree to bloom all summer can be grouped with daffodils for winter flowers with space left over for annual plantings such as pansies in fall and petunias in spring.

Azalea garden in spring.

Get to know natives. The term 'native plant' differs in definition, but natives have begun to make a stronger showing at the garden center than last century for good reason. Their beauty brings out the best in a locality and evokes that treasured sense of place. Whether you care if a plant is native to your county alone, or to a larger geographic area, you're probably already growing some. It is important to realize that your garden is not likely to be a match for their natural habitat. Their adaptability is legend, but be reasonable—bog plants native to the nearby swamp won't grow well if you simply plop them into an established xeriscape garden bed for plants that like it dry. Native plants are valuable for their inherent beauty and durable performance, but they have another benefit. Most are grown near where you live, further ensuring the odds they'll do well for you. Shopping for natives often allows you to meet and support the local growers and plant aficionados who can be valuable resources of garden smarts and friendship as well as plants.

Louisiana iris

Plant at least one thing you just love. Gardening can be a very personal journey, if you do it right. Maybe you strike out and try things, or maybe you read volumes and ask questions before you begin. It doesn't matter the way the garden teaches you, for as the old saying goes, "When the student is ready, the teacher appears." Plenty of people will tell you not to even try to grow certain plants in a particular area, and in general, they are right. I say listen to the naysayers so you'll know the pitfalls, but go ahead. If you want to try plant X in place Y, or try to get something you love to adapt by giving it extra TLC, it might work and you'll certainly learn something even if it doesn't. There comes a day for everybody who gardens when the place looks good even to your own critical eye. On that day, the weirdo plant shines amid everything else and your journey progresses a couple more steps. Take pictures in case it doesn't happen again.

Get organized and keep a neat edge on everything. As a voracious plant collector, I have at times created gardens no one but me could love and understand. Over time I have learned to segregate the plants I'm growing from the ones I am maintaining. Both are equally exciting at times, but they need different care regimes and can look very confusing together, especially in a container garden. Visualize asparagus roots with fern spilling out of a crate sitting next to a carefully groomed peace lily and you'll know what I mean. I have also learned not to put the plants I'm unsure of in the front garden. If they drop dead, I want to be the first to know. Organizing may be a simple matter of deciding that you'll water the front garden in the morning, and containers on the deck at the same time you water the backyard. Or it might mean staging the plants in a bed so they bloom in sequence or simultaneously at different heights. No matter what you plant, a neat edge around beds and along paths makes everything look better all the time. It may be an illusion, but even the weeds look better when the beds they're in have a well-maintained edge.

Embrace the rule of trey. Three may be the most useful number in planting the garden. Three tomato plants generously feed a family of four. One flower pot on a windowsill always reminds me of Humpty Dumpty all alone and waiting to fall. Two are even less interesting to me, but a trio of pots instantly makes a scene. Choose two or three different sizes of similar shape or color and set them two side by side with the third in front. Whatever plants you choose, three pots together simply sing. Three elements make up classic flower arranging, and readily translate to mixed containers and garden bed arrangements. Of course, I have my own names for the three essentials.

Headdress. Think of this element as the soaring feathers atop the incredible costumes of the Mardi Gras Indians. Every combination of plants needs an upright element of inspiration, just as ponds need plants at their margin to lead the eye from earth to sky. This crown of the scene can be its spiky punctuation mark or an effusive burst of upright stems, but in every case it is what catches your eye first.

Bodice. The centerpiece of the arrangement is what holds your interest. A flowering plant or one with unusual leaf patterns fills the center and if it also has strong texture, so much the better. Without the continuity this element provides, the planting will look strangely disconnected; with it, the grouping will be consistently good looking.

Skirt. If you've ever watched serious square dancers, you've seen rick rack, the wide, zigzag edging that gives the ladies the look of a spinning top as it moves. Beneath that are the petticoats, white eyelet and gathered to hold the skirt aloft. Both these images are what I call the skirt of any plant group. The wide world of frilly, trailing plants can frame the bodice or hug the soil beneath it. Softer texture here helps to ease the transition from soil to plants and keep them visually grounded.

Don't overdo diversity. With all this talk of planting to enhance your garden's attractiveness to beneficial insects and harmless critters of all sorts, keep balance in mind. Plant enough of one species to make a show, just plant lots of species over all. A wild mix of colors makes any area look smaller, while a solid bed of red looks larger. There's no geometry involved, just visual perception. Mix the two notions to express yourself in different ways, even within the same bed. Let it begin with one color, say red impatiens, to line the walk up to your door. Where the bed opens up at the landing, put in a mix of colors. The solid red will move eyes and feet to the splash of colors accenting the destination.

Pick a color to call your own and a word for your garden style. These last two lessons are mine in this decade and can guide us all to smarter choices in plants and gardening practices. Somehow green just isn't enough for me anymore, though it's been my favorite color all my life. I want an accent color to use throughout the gardens as a unifying element, as the pros call it. To me, it's more like planting the flag. When I finally decide on The Color, hopefully in this decade, I will use it to mark the little bits of Earth I am grateful to steward: the fence in Jackson, pots and furniture in Baton Rouge, a trellis in New Orleans. Finding this color is part of the ongoing process of ultimately defining my garden style. It may sound strange, but I don't know what word describes the looks of my plantings. Maybe your cottage garden is charming or if you've assembled a collection of yard art, perhaps your style is whimsical.

~~~

My gardens are, and always have been, plants contained in beds, pots, and greenhouses. I only know that am a devotee of plants. I buy them, accept them as gifts, propagate and grow them from seed, and try not to kill them. I honestly believe that seeing the next flower bloom is my reward for making it through another day, another week, another season. My garden has been described as eccentric, comfortable, and interesting, by various visitors, and I grow most of the species on Neil Odenwald's list describing 'southern romantic garden plants. To me, it's a garden in the key of my life, and that's enough.

<u>Garden Notes</u>

Our Gardening Calendar

Here we go through the year, with ideas on when to do what, weather permitting, and extra space for your own entries.

~~~January~~~

Focus on fruit. Plant new fruit trees now and prune established ones. Grow what you want to take care of! Not willing to establish a spray routine? Stick to figs, blueberries, feijoa, and natal plums. Peaches, plums, apples and the like will need regular sprays to avoid predictable insects and diseases.

Summer investment. Cut down chaste tree and butterfly bush if they got thickety last fall or prune out their dead wood and clip back what you leave on the trees.

Vine time. Prune muscadine grapes and wisteria this month. Leave the big canes alone, but look for the side shoots that come off of them. Clip the side shoots to two inches.

Grass chance. Before the new growth starts, cut back last year's leaves of ornamental grasses (maiden, fountain, pampas et al) and clumping ground covers that are also grasses or grasslike (liriope, monkey, mondo and the like). The large perennial grasses must be cut down completely to their crowns, and the groundcovers can be cut down, too, for rejuvenation. Or just trim the worn out leaves off the ground covers. Part the clumps to see if new shoots are up, and do not cut back sharply if so.

Food action. Start broccoli, cabbage, and lettuce seeds indoors ASAP for transplant a few weeks later. Three critical factors rule seedling success: a fresh bag of sterile seed starting mix, ample light close to the plants, and your ability to water seed pots or pellets from the bottom. Control these elements and you can sprout anything. Label it all!

~~~February~~~

Focus on roses. Prune shrub roses by mid-month, climbers not at all until after they bloom. Vigorous shrub roses can be pruned to 3 feet to control their size and maintain good air circulation around each plant. Remove any twiggy or dead canes now, too, and spread compost under each one.

Get 'em. Take a wet day walk and pull weeds out while they're seedlings and the soil is soft. A long-handled, sharp pointed tool works well for this task, such as a keen hoe or Cobrahead tool.

Food for thought. Plant potatoes early, other early spring vegetable seedlings on the first nice day. Sow seeds of nasturtium, carrot, beet, swiss chard, mustard, collard, and turnip directly into the garden.

Evergreener. Begin clipping hedges and shaping tree-form evergreens. A few inches off all around each spring as new growth begins keeps plants thick and their height controlled. Prune berried shrubs right after the birds finish their feast to prepare the plants for new flowers and next year's bounty.

Mow for less. Get the flowers off those winter lawn weeds before they can make more seed. Crank up the mower or use the grass shears, but do it. Compost flowers and leaves that you have clipped off, but burn or trash any other plant parts that you remove, such as roots and above ground runners.

~~~March~~~

Afterbloom. Prune flowering shrubs within a month after they bloom. Quince and witch hazel should already have been shaped up, camellias, too. Don't miss the azaleas, which can be trimmed all over like the other popular shrubs. When canes get bigger around than your thumb, they dominate and can stifle the new growth that keeps the shrub tidy and flowerful. Cut out the huge ones and let the young ones flourish.

Split search. Check the stems on shrubs if the winter was harsh. Cracks in them now may mean sudden death this summer. Prune at least a few inches off the damaged shrub to reduce its stress, and keep an eye on it.

Resist the push. Shop for annuals you can plant within a week of purchase. That means lay off the vinca and impatiens until your soil warms up, but go for spring's best, like petunias and all their relatives. Buy caladiums and start them indoors in pots if the spring is cool and wet.

Dig it. As hostas and other summer perennials pop up, it's time to dig, divide, and replant. Cast iron plant and Lenten rose, too, can use your attention now, even though they're well up and leafy by now. Generally, divide perennials in the opposite season from their bloom, but if the spring is cold, wet, and short, you can usually safely delay until fall. The reverse is true, too, when the fall is hot and dry right up to the first freeze. You may lose or delay flowers, but this process is all about the long term health of the plants. Ultimately, that brings more flowers.

Small starts. Plant big containers full of small starter plants now and grow them to the grandeur of a professionally planted mixed pot. Remember the rule of trey as you put these pots together, and don't forget to water regularly and fertilize often.

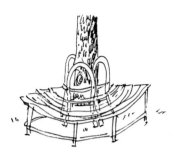

~~~April~~~

Shape up. Nandinas, too, benefit from occasional rejuvenation to let in sun and water to spur more canes. Clip out the oldest or those with only a few leaflets either at the top or the bottom of the cane.

Pick it. Keep strawberries and leaf lettuces picked to extend the harvest. Watch for spider mites and leaf spots on both these crops.

Let go. Daffodils and other bulbs use their leaves after flowering to transfer nutrients to their underground heart. Don't mow until they're at least half browned.

Shear joy. Vining ground covers like Asiatic jasmine and perennial vinca can be trimmed back by a few inches now to keep them lush. Fertilize them to keep their mats thick. Cut back once blooming, climbing roses like 'Lady Banksia' when flowers fade.

Repot the lot. As you move the indoor containers outside, move up and give new soil to any that you'd like to really grow during the summer. Don't step up from a small pot to a huge one unless you want to wait weeks for new top growth to begin. If roots are hopelessly crowded, separate if possible and prune if necessary to settle them into the new soil and promote new rooting.

~~~May~~~

Reap and keep. Harvest parsley and cilantro before they bolt and freeze some for future use. Fill ice cube trays with washed, destemmed leaves, covered with water. Once frozen, crack the cubes into a plastic bag and store for soups and marinades.

Eyes up. Plant caladium bulbs with their nose, or eye, up. That's where the first leaves emerge. Dahlia tubers, though, need room to spread out. Dig a hole to plant them in and backfill it to form a mound. Center the dahlia on top of the mound, spread its small tubers onto its sides, then add soil all around and on top of it.

Hot stuff. Seeds like okra, moonflower, and four o'clock and sweet potato slips start faster and make a stronger stand when planted in very warm soil. Soak large seeds in warm water for a few hours to soften their coats and speed sprouting.

For more even seeding of smaller seeds, like cleome, fill a salt shaker with sand, add seeds, and sprinkle into place.

Pare down. Thin the fruit on pear, plum, and other fruits now to allow the rest to ripen without breaking branches because of the weight of the load. Find ways to keep birds and squirrels off ripening fruit. Use distractions such as mirrors and wind chimes, but change their places weekly to keep 'em confused. Put nets on, but don't anchor them so tightly that they become ladders! Better to buy larger nets and suspend them just above the plants.

Frond fun. Soak hanging fern baskets weekly in a bucket of water mixed with half-strength fertilizer to meet their serious need for hydration.

Pepper power. Once warm weather is well under way, give peppers plenty of water and fertilizer to get them growing. Pick off the earliest peppers as soon as they are ripe and keep picking. Remember, anytime you let the fruit linger on the plant, it will set seed inside and stop making more peppers.

Smart steps. Don't let fears of west nile virus and skin cancer cut into your garden time. Protect yourself by wearing effective repellent and sunscreen every time you go outside. And, if you don't remember the last time you had a tetanus shot, it's likely time for this once-a-decade inoculation.

~~~June~~~

Lawn smarts. Know what is and isn't a problem by insisting on a correct diagnosis. Moles may not need to be trapped if you control the tasty grubs living in the soil. Browned areas might be chinch bugs, might be brown patch or take-all root rot fungus diseases. In rare cases it can indicate a natural gas leak underground. If you smell gas or cannot diagnose the reason for the browning, call your utility company.

Bam ready. Dig up garlic, onion, shallot, and multiplying onion for kitchen use and to save sets for fall planting. Separate, shake the dirt off, and store out of direct sun with good air circulation.

Pinched up. Coleus and other plants with square stems like mint, garden mums, and fall perennials like joe pye weed can and should be pinched this month. Bushier plants and more flowers will result, and the pinches will root, too, if you want more.

Slug patrol. Forget beer traps. Use a copper ring or copper paste around vulnerable plants, pull back the mulch, or set up a banana trap instead. Lean a board on a brick, put a banana peel underneath, and scoop up all the slugs the next day.

Water wise. During drought years, water lawns, shrubs and trees weekly, but soak, don't sprinkle. Infrequent, slow waterings that percolate into the soil are most effective.

~~~July~~~

Deadheads. Remove spent blooms from flowering annuals, perennials, shrubs, and trees unless you want them to go to seed. If you want to encourage new seedlings of Mexican hat, cosmos, or zinnia, rake their mulch back so fallen seeds can make good soil contact.

Sooty looks. A black film on leaves or lawn furniture means that sucking insects are feeding somewhere near. Clean the film off with soapy water and stifle the bugs if it's practical.

Wilt nots. Do not fertilize, spray, or cut plants that are water stressed. Presoak them one day, or in the morning, then get busy. Pick herbs, flowers, and especially vegetables and fruits early in the day. That is when their flavors and colors are most concentrated.

Jackie O. Plant pumpkins before Independence Day to have eating and decorating fruit ready in October. Don't forget to plant a reservoir alongside huge vines like pumpkin and gourds. Whether they are called miniature, birdhouse, or luffa sponge, give those pumkins and gourds lots of room and ready access to water and fertilizer.

Harvest Ahead. Get fall tomatoes and broccoli planted this month. You can root tomato suckers from existing plants, start seeds, or buy transplants of heat

resistant varieties of 'maters and broccoli. To avoid heat stress, provide shade for the young plants with twigs or old window screens set up between them and the late afternoon sun. Set up a sprinkler on a timer for a midday misting to prevent the 'swoon and wilt' syndrome that can stunt these young plants.

Blight now. If powdery mildew continues on crepe myrtle, prune out just the damaged parts. But if fire blight has turned whole branches of Bradford or fruiting pears black, make cuts several inches back into the healthy wood in hopes of slowing the spread of the blight.

~~~August~~~

Pea mine. Last call to plant lady, cream, purple hull, and other southern peas for the fall season. Lots of warm season crops can be planted now, like squash and beans. Consult local recommendations for last dates for planting. Prepare a spot to plant spinach next month by raising its pH: work in lime or crushed eggshells now and let them set awhile.

Dark side. Cut down tough vines and invasive plants when the new moon arrives in August. This is old-time advice that works to suppress their return.

Air play. Houseplants with sturdy stems that are overgrown can be air layered now. Make a slit in the stem, wedge it open with a toothpick, and wrap the whole area with wet sphagnum moss. Seal it up with clear plastic tied onto the stem at top and bottom of the moss lump. Cut the stem off when rooted to make a second plant and reduce the size of the mama.

Grass rush. The last, best time to plant lawns from seed is now. Get the summer weeds out first by scraping them off with a sharpened spade, then turn the soil, rake smooth, and use a seeder, not your fist, for even seed distribution.

Seed sensations. Sow flower and vegetable seed for plants to set out next month: beautiful sweet William, poppy, candytuft, calendula, foxglove, and hollyhock. Sure, you can grow your own pansies and snapdragons, but since those overwintering annuals are readily available, why not try something new?

~~~September~~~

Trim time. Use hedge shears or the string trimmer to cut back beds of annuals and perennials gone wrong. Impatiens, lantana, verbena, and petunias will bloom again before frost.

Do shrubs. Fall trimming of evergreen hedges neatens them up and suppresses rampant shoots. Keep an eye out for browned juniper branches and rake up underneath. Might be spider mites, might not, but clean up is first. Add these shrubs to the list for oil spray in December.

Bag it. To safely collect seed from plants that crack open and shoot them everywhere, tie small paper bag around their necks. When the seeds fly, you've got them bagged.

Get ready. Prepare the soil now for fall shrub, tree, and bulb planting. Practice good garden sanitation as leaves fall, and turn the compost as you add new ingredients.

Patchwork. Dig up areas of lawn and ground cover that just didn't make it this year. Work the soil lightly, add compost, and plant sprigs or clumps taken from across the yard or buy some new plants.

~~~October~~~

Cut circles. To ready trees and shrubs for transplant, use a shovel to cut a circle as far out from the trunk as you expect to be able to dig up the plant. Roots will begin to grow inside the circle, and you'll dig it up with less transplant shock.

Pot march. Head 'em up, and move 'em in. Take a good look at houseplants, send the lizards and rolypolies to another part of the garden, and wash leaves before moving them indoors. Time it so they're inside at least two weeks before you turn on heaters.

Trash and treasure. Clear the weeds out from around clumping ground covers not quite grown together yet, and weed around perennials as they go dormant. Don't compost weeds gone to seed, or you might see them again.

Rye gains. New house, no lawn yet? Sow perennial ryegrass seed this month for erosion control, gorgeous green color, and efficient roots that contribute to soil structure.

Empty bed. If you've prepared a bed for spring planting already or have a bed empty for another reason, give it green manure. Sow seed leftover from the current or past year, then turn it under when it reaches four inches tall for a natural nitrogen boost.

~~~November~~~

Eating in. Fertilize overwintering annuals monthly unless it's freezing to keep flowers and vegetables growing. Adapt that screen box: recover it with 6 mil clear plastic sheeting and it becomes a cold frame.

Leaf matters. To speed the compost process, rake leaves into ankle deep piles and mow them. Don't miss the leaves that fall onto shrubs and tree hollows.

Daffy days. Plant bulbs now: daffodil, grape hyacinth, giant allium, plus anemone and ranunculus if you dare. Leave the tulips and hyacinths in the refrigerator for now.

Table scents. Start forcing bulbs now for gifts and holiday decorating. Nestle paperwhites into gravel that you've watered once. Put the pot in the dark and water weekly until the shoots are four inches tall. Give bright light and more water to force into bloom.

Afterbloom. Red spider lilies and sasanqua trees, candelabra plant and cardinal flower have finished blooming for the year. Fertilize lily clumps, prune sasanqua within a month of bloom, collect seed from candelabra and cut back cardinal flower and other perennials.

~~~December~~~

Bulb up. Fertilize bulb clumps soon after the leaves appear. This goes for the entire group, from daffodils to cannas, which won't sprout for weeks yet.

Crown jewels. Clean up around perennials to remove plant debris and be sure mulch isn't choking the crown. Removing browned stems now will keep them from becoming fungus hotels if the winter is wet.

Oily friends. Get to know oil sprays and use them properly on trees and shrubs. Reserve dormant oils for fruit trees, and use only horticultural, highly refined oils on all else.

Keep going. Put covers on the lettuce, or thank whoever built your cold frame so the salad greens can be fresh all year. Know that collards and Brussels sprouts improve in taste with chilly weather.

Greenhouse gifts. Feed your passion for gardening by asking for a greenhouse as a gift, or a new deck, potting bench, or a sunroom. Give and get what you need: huge containers and a pressure sprayer, plus waterproof clogs, straw hats, sunscreen and insect repellants.

Wrapped up. Gift plants need good drainage. Remove wrapping to water, and when you do, let water go through the pot and out into the sink. Dry it and replace the decorations. Don't water again until the top of the soil feels just dry. Put poinsettia, christmas cactus, gardenia, and others in bright light away from direct sun, heating vents, and doors to the outside that are opened frequently.

Fresh cuts. Hope you ordered greenery from the local nonprofit group that sells it, but don't stop there. Just like you cut fresh flowers for the table, cut berried branches, dried hydrangea blooms, and evergreen magnolia and bring the best of the outdoors in. Get into the gold spray paint or white flocking, add candles and be festive.

The Plants In My Gardens, and The Ones I Wish I Had

My definition of a superior plant is one I like that grows with less effort than I gain from its joys. A wise friend once told me that the way to determine if a long-term relationship is failing is to take a count of the good weeks and bad weeks. If the bad outweighs the good by two to one for more than a year and you aren't a martyr, it's time to do something. So it is with the plants on this list. They have stood the test of time with much more joy than irritation.

I've included plants native to the Southeast and also plants called exotic because they aren't from around here—the Southerner cliché said of any person transplanted to their town for less than twenty years. My own favorite roses and warm season turf grasses are included elsewhere in this book, but are certainly a part of my gardens. The same is true with countless annuals, herbs, and veggies. It's easy to try new choices of these each year. Few roses and turfs, if any, are native where we live, but I cannot imagine the garden without the ones that grow and behave as well as any native plant might.

A few plants in each huge category are also invasive and should never be planted because they crowd out desirable species. Some exotics, such as azalea and crepe myrtle, have grown here for generations, though, becoming integral parts of our plant palette. Who could imagine spring without daffodils?

These days a plant list can easily offend someone with other views about what should be grown and even what is native to where. I suggest that you consider the plants on my list, and then if you like, argue with me and make your own list, native or not. There are plenty more plants that thrive in the Deep South in addition to these, but as a group, this bunch makes a fine garden with year round interest and wildlife sustenance. Unless otherwise noted, they require only routine watering once established, that is, an occasional deep soak when rain isn't consistent, and moderate amounts of fertilizer.

A final caveat about the list: if you find that any plant, found here or anywhere, becomes listed as invasive in your area, don't plant it or its close relatives. Remove what you have and destroy, do not compost, them. That being said, a rampant plant is not necessarily invasive and can be very useful in filling space without resorting to more turf, for example, than you'd like to manage.

Key To Plant Descriptions
W= wetland native, provide consistent moisture
D = drought tolerant once established
S = sunny sites preferred
SS = some sun ok, some shade ok, too
SH = shade preferred
E = evergreen; F = flowers; C = fall color;
B = berries/nuts; N = SE native plant

LARGE LANDSCAPE TREES

Beech *(Fagus grandiflora)*   SS, C, N

A moderate grower to 70 feet in acid soil with good drainage, the beech tree delivers reliable, strong yellow fall color. Plant in the open for its huge, shady canopy and beechnuts (no relation to the famous gum). The nuts appeal to wildlife, birds, and squirrels, and the wood is preferred by furniture makers and artisans for its strength and turning ability.

Big Leaf Magnolia *(Magnolia macrophylla)* SS, F, N

Noted for leaves as long as your arm, this is a slow grower reaching 30-50 feet in height eventually. Among the very oldest magnolias, it sports gigantic fragrant flowers attractive to its beetle pollinators. Plant in organically rich, well-drained soil where prevailing winds won't tear its leaves, in partial shade or full sun. Not very drought tolerant. The leaves are great in arrangements and crafts.

Black Walnut *(Juglans nigra)*   S, F, B, N

A vigorous, 70+ foot shade tree native to forests along damp river bottoms that can also be grown in full sun. Its wood is prized and its nuts favored by wildlife and people, but litter limits its use to the backyard. The roots exude juglone, a chemical that suppresses other plant growth, so grow it alone. Juglone is not harmful to people or other wildlife.

Catalpa *(Catalpa bignonioides)*   S, F, N

30 x 30 feet or taller and fast growing, this beautiful flowering tree is a bit brittle and messy, but well worth the labor. Heart shaped leaves appear before the bloom clusters of white bells marked

inside with purple and orange. My grandfather fished for bream with the larvae of the sphinx moth, aka Catawba worms, that feed on its leaves.

Crepe myrtle *(Lagerstroemia indica and others)* S, D, F

Ranging in mature height from three to 30 feet, the southern lilac (I hate that name!) is well covered in elsewhere in the book. See pages 86 to 88.

Nellie Stevens Holly *(Ilex x Nellie Stevens)* S, SS, E, B

Though not named for me, this is my favorite evergreen holly. It is the most reliable in our warmest climates, and grows to 25 feet and half as wide. Its best features include medium green leaves with nice thorns and triad berries nestled in their tips. Superior drainage and mostly sunny sites are favored, and growth is moderately fast. Recently released cultivars with Nellie in their background are worth a close look, too.

Red Bay *(Persea borbonia)* W, SH, E, N

This tree grows at a moderate rate to upwards of 70 feet, and while it is native to swamp borders, will grow well in light shade anywhere in the Southeast. Give it rich, fertile soil with decent drainage and it will grow to be fairly drought tolerant. Its amazingly fragrant leaves substitute well for its Laurel family relative and European native, bay leaf laurel.

Red Maple *(Acer rubrum)* W, S, SS, C, N

50 feet tall on average, moderate growth rate, and displaying great color and form, this upright tree grows in wet or well-drained soils. When the red maple blooms and the new red leaves emerge in winter high over the Atchafalaya Swamp, I am reassured that Mardi Gras is here and spring will follow.

Southern magnolia *(Magnolia grandiflora)* S, D, F, E, N

Perhaps the grande dame of our region, this tree grows slowly to 80 feet with huge trunks and branches that drape to ground level if you let them. The creamy ivory flowers reek with musk and are most abundant when trees are grown on sunny sites in well-drained soil. For smaller gardens, choose Little Gem and other dwarf cultivars.

111

Favorite Oaks

The finest legacy to leave your grandchildren and your community might be oak trees (*Quercus* species). 60 species are native to the USA, and another 150 to Mexico, a substantial percentage of the 600 total *Quercus* species worldwide. These are my favorites, in this order.

Live Oak *(Q. virginiana)*   S, C, N

For coastal areas and sandy soils inland through zone 8. Never underestimate the size of the tree you plant; at maturity this one needs 80 feet between it and anything else. The spreading canopy and draping branches may not grow fast, but the future depends on our investment in this and other noble trees.

This grand live oak shades the whole neighborhood.

Red Oak *(Northern red is Q. rubra, Southern red is Q. falcata)* S, C, N

Fast for oaks, this one adds two feet a year and acorns in a relatively short 20 years. Northern red is best in upper zone 8 and 7; Southern red grows everywhere else and tolerates heavier soils. Almost evergreen, the new leaves seem to push the old ones off. Cherrybark oak (*Q. falcata* var. *pagodifolia)* is best for bottomlands such as the Mississippi Delta.

W-wetland; D-drought tolerant; S-sun preferred; SS-some sun, some shade; SH-shade preferred; E-evergreen; F-flowers; C-fall color; B-berries; N-Southeast native plant.

Water Oak *(Q. nigra)*   S, C, N

Confusingly named perhaps, the native water oak is not a wetland tree and does not tolerate flooding. It is not as long lived but is faster growing than most oaks. It is best planted away from structures in a group of trees. Its spatula-shaped leaves make excellent compost.

water oak

White Oak *(Quercus alba)*   S, C, N

White oaks reach 20 feet in 15 years. Then growth slows down yet trees reach 80 feet at maturity. It has a wide canopy of deeply cut leaves in a classic oakleaf shape. An essential part of the hardwood forest, it prefers slightly acid soil.

Overcup Oak *(Q. lyrata)*   SS, SH, C, N

A moderate grower to 60 feet, the overcup oak (left) is is a good urban tree with a neat habit and tolerance of most soil conditions. It has warm cocoa fall color and great acorns with big knobby caps.

Chinkapin Oak *(Q. muehlenbergii)*   W, S, SH, N

A slow grower to 60 feet and a favorite in acid soil, this one is a sentimental favorite. Named for leaves shaped like those of a chestnut, it displays good red or warm brown fall color.

Nuttall Oak *(Q. nuttallii)* & Shumard *(Q. shumardii)* S, C, N

Closely allied oaks, the Nuttalls tolerate wetter sites and develop mature form sooner than other species. Both are moderate growers to 50-70 feet in about as many years. They sport strong fall color.

Willow Oak *(Q. phellos)*   W, S, SS, C, N

A moderate grower, the willow oak eventually reaches 70 feet with a dense canopy of narrow, bright green leaves. It is fairly tolerant of damp soils.

Basket Oak *(Q. prinus)*   S, C, N

This one is also known as the Chestnut oak because its leaves are evenly waved and sort of resemble its namesake. It is a moderate grower to 50 feet which does best in acid soils and is lauded for basketweaving and fence wattling.

Small Trees

Althea *(Hibiscus sinensis)*   **S, SS, F**

Growing to 15 feet tall, this tree has multiple stems emerging from its base and sprouts matte green leaves densely along each branch. Some forms are very upright, other more widely spread, and the large flowers range from white through pink and red to purple. Althea grows in any soil, but it blooms more if pruned in the summer for shape and irrigated during dry seasons.

Chaste tree *(Vitex agnes-castus)*   **S, F**

The first time I saw this tree I nearly ran off the road admiring it. It has a rounded shape and grows rapidly to 12 to 15 feet. It looks best pruned with multiple low branches coming up from a short, stocky trunk. Summer brings stunning blue flowers held in upright pyramids when it is grown in well-drained garden soil. Prune this tree hard in early spring to avoid a thickety form.

Fringetree *(Chionanthes virginicus)*   **S, SS, F, C, N**

Also known as Grancy Greybeard, this 20-foot tree thrives in good drainage and makes a fine addition to beds or lawns for spring flowers and neat habit. Clusters of thin tubular flowers appear all over the tree before the leaves emerge. Their arrangement and color against dark gray bark gives rise to both common names.

Japanese maple *(Acer palmatum)*   **SS, C**

With rapid growth to 15 feet tall and five feet wide, this tree has finely cut leaves and can be pruned to accentuate its linear form. Depending on variety, classic maple leaf shapes emerge red. Some turn green in summer but some do not. Either way they they redden again in fall. Excellent drainage is imperative, and some shade and protection from prevailing winds will benefit leaf color and stability.

Parsley Haw *(Crataegus marshallii)*   **S, SS, F, C, N**

Named for its leaf shape resembling clusters of very dark green flat leaf parsley, this native should be included in many more gardens. A shapely tree growing to

W-wetland; D-drought tolerant; S-sun preferred; SS-some sun, some shade; SH-shade preferred; E-evergreen; F-flowers; C-fall color; B-berries; N-Southeast native plant.

15 feet tall, it is great for the back of the border or as a focal point. It is adaptable to most southern soils. Its flowers are tiny and white, appearing in spring.

Possum Haw *(Ilex decidua)*   D, S, B, N

Unparalleled for winter form and color, this tree can be grown as a single 20-foot trunk or allowed to thicket wildly. The holly loses its small green leaves to reveal the shiniest scarlet red berries of the winter garden, and they are a late season bird food favorite. Adaptable to most conditions, it grows best in sun where the soil drains well.

Red Buckeye *(Aesculus pavia)*   SS, F, N

A special favorite for the hummingbirds it attracts, this tree soon reaches 12 by 12 feet with plentiful red flower spikes. The leaflets are arranged like fans, repeating the charming flower's strong points. Native to the forest understory, it is best grown in a similar organically rich soil. The seeds are dark brown with tan spots and carried for luck.

Southern crabapple *(Malus angustifolia)*   SS, F, B, N

The sweet pink 'crab' jelly of my childhood comes from the fruit of this native tree with splotchy but attractive gray bark. Pink and white flower clusters look like their cousins, the fresh eating apples, but yield clusters of small, hard fruit favored by wildlife. The tree grows rapidly to 20 feet in lightly shaded places in well-drained soil. It is not drought tolerant.

Sweet Olive *(Osmanthus fragrans)*   S, SS, E, F

For months of deliciously sweet flowers at your doorstep, plant this small tree or large shrub next to any entrance that gets half a day of sun. With annual pruning when new growth starts in the spring, its growth stays compact. Without it, a natural legginess is not unattractive. Adaptable to all but the sandiest soil, the tree grows slowly in heavy, unamended clay soil.

Wax myrtle *(Myrica cerifera)*   S, SS, E, B

Usually multi-trunked, this tree forms a colony if suckers coming from the roots are not controlled. Very tolerant of conditions throughout the South, this native is an essential wildlife plant noted for its waxy, high-protein berries. It is able to fix nitrogen from the air, like beans and peas, so it can be grown in difficult soils.

Fruits and Nuts

Banana *(Musa* species) S, F

You can grow a 20-foot 'Basjoo', hardiest of the bananas, for tropical texture, not for eating. The same goes for 'Bordelon', the maroon blotched banana plant. To eat, 'Dwarf Orinoco' is only eight feet tall with very long leaves and large tasty bananas; it is hardy to Zone 7b; 'Ice Cream' is hardy well into Zone 8 with delicious white fruit. Cut down the stalks and mulch the crowns well in late fall.

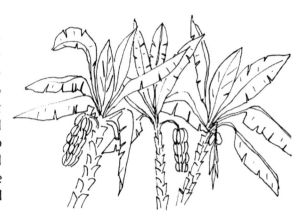

Blueberry *(Vaccinium* species) S, SS, E, B, F, N

Of all the attractive kinds of fruit for home cultivation, blueberries fit into the landscape best, with fine spring flowers, summer fruit for the birds if you don't like it yourself, and striking fall color. It rapidly reaches six plus feet in sun, and should be pruned to shape after fruiting. This one grows in acid soil, rich in organic matter and well drained. Mulch well; these are shallow roots.

Fig *(Ficus carica)* S, F

Among the oldest fruit in the fossil record, figs may be the easiest home garden fruit to try. A fig tree will develop a spreading canopy to 20 if left unpruned, but should be cut back in January to control excess height. Choose local favorite varieties for most success; some bear one crop a year, others two. Grow in rich organic soils and mulch deeply.

Japanese Persimmon *(Diospyros kaki)* S, C, F

The persimmon is an excellent landscape tree noted for fall color and fruit. These exotic Japanese persimmons have been grown here since the 1890's. There are two types: astringent 'Tananashi' which will make you pucker if you eat them before they get soft, and non-astringent 'Fuyo', the world's favorite for fresh eating. Freeze ripe fruits whole for a custard-style treat.

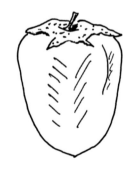

W-wetland; D-drought tolerant; S-sun preferred; SS-some sun, some shade; SH-shade preferred; E-evergreen; F-flowers; C-fall color; B-berries; N-Southeast native plant.

Loquat *(Eriobotrya japonica)*   S, SS, F, B

Gardens farthest south will harvest the most fruit, but the loquat is a lovely small garden tree anywhere. Averaging 12 feet tall and five feet wide at the crown, its stiff dark green leaves are almost puckered and quite rough looking for a tropical touch in courtyards. The fruits are delicious, grape-textured sweet treats that look a little like small peaches. Grow this in well-drained soil and mulch well. Named cultivars bear the best fruit.

Mayhaw *(Crataegus opaca)*   W, S, F, B, N

The best jelly that ever met a biscuit comes from berries on these slow growing trees, known as mayhaws, which are Southern hawthornes. The red fruit will be plentiful if pollinated so plant at least two trees. Ample water in well-drained garden soil on sunny sites works best for fruit production, even though the trees are native to low, wet areas. Whether for wildlife or family food, this is a great garden tree.

Paw Paw *(Asimina triloba)*   S, SS, C, N

Yes, you can pick up paw paws and put 'em in your pocket, as the old song says. The fruits taste remarkably like banana custard with pineapple undertones. Its a 25-foot shade tree, too, giving a definite tropical look to the garden. Particularly dependent on the soil food web for nutrition, paw paw demands an organically rich, well-drained soil.

Persimmon *(Diospyros virginiana)*   S, SS, C, F, N

This native tree reaches 25 feet with small, pumpkin-perfect orange fruit in fall dotting its dark gray branches. A widely adapted and essential wildlife food plant, it is best used at the edges of woodland gardens and on fencerows. It is not as drought tolerant as *D. kaki.*

Pecan *(Carya illinoensis)* S, C, B, N

Grand, legacy trees, plant a pecan for its long life as a shade tree and for nuts, if you have room for a pollinator tree or the neighbor happens to grow a different variety. A bearing pecan is a joy, but it has other benefits, including distinctive, avocado green leaves that shatter and decompose rapidly in the compost. Experts tell you pecans are impractical for home gardens because of their pest control needs. However, plenty of people grow pecans, particularly newer varieties that are more pest resistant such as 'Elliott', 'Candy', and in coastal areas, 'Jackson'.

Satsuma *(Citrus species)*   **S, F**

Satsumas are small rounded trees to 12 feet high, with mandarin-orange shaped fruits. This is the hardiest citrus for home gardens. Give these trees excellent soil drainage and regular summer watering to ripen 'LA Early' and 'Early St. Ann' in September, and 'Owari' for harvest from October to frost. Hardiness is improved further south, but still they are a very good bet in Zone 8.

Shagbark Hickory *(Carya ovata)*   **SS, C, B, N**

Huge trees, shagbark hickories grow to 70 feet tall and 40 feet wide with striking gray bark. These hardwoods have the best hickory nuts. Unfortunately, it takes half a century to produce many nuts. In the meantime, this is a dramatic tree for woodland mixed plantings and big backyards in any well-drained soil. Like its relative the pecan, this is a legacy shade tree with nuts as a bonus.

Strawberry guava *(Psidium cattleianum)*   **S, F, E**

Reliably hardy to 25 degrees F., this very adaptable shrub makes an excellent container plant where it must be protected. Waxy leaves, thick growth in a neat habit, and excellent, strawberry-flavored fruit make it a good choice for home fruit growing where space is limited. It can reach 20 feet, but can be kept much smaller or pruned to tree form.

Shrubs

Arrowwood *(Viburnum dentatum 'Osceola')* S, SS, F, N

Plant several arrowwoods for a sturdy wildlife thicket. They grow eight by eight feet with dark leaves and creamy flowers in late spring followed by inky blue fruit. As the name indicates this shrub is a source of shaft wood for arrows. This family deserves much more attention for its native and exotic members well-suited to heat and humidity. Farther south, Chippewa viburnum and Chinese snowball viburnum have many fans.

W-wetland; D-drought tolerant; S-sun preferred; SS-some sun, some shade; SH-shade preferred; E-evergreen; F-flowers; C-fall color; B-berries; N-Southeast native plant.

Azaleas *(Rhododendron species)* SS, F, E

Reblooming or spring singles, mainly hybrids

Long time acid-loving favorites for big spring flower shows and repeat performances much of the year. Prune both types right after first bloom and follow with fertilizer.

Native azaleas   SS, F

Leafless while flowers amaze, many are fragrant and best suited for slightly more shade than the evergreens. Excellent drainage in rich organic soils with mulch benefit these.

Banana shrub *(Michelia figo)*   SS, F, E

At home in the South since before 1800, the fragrant banana shrub grows well with azaleas and camellias. Its flowers are smaller, and while noted for a banana aroma, it is truly closer to a banana liqueur or banana sno cone smell. It is not fast growing, but is long lived in organic soils. It's not drought tolerant in sunny sites.

Beautyberry *(Callicarpa americana)*   S, SS, B, N

Callicarpa rapidly reaches six feet tall and almost as wide, and matures at over ten feet if left unpruned. It is an understory plant with arching stems and it forms an exuberant vase in the piney woods, but also is excellent in garden soil in some shade. It is fairly drought tolerant. Its spring flowers are OK but are followed by outstanding chains of shiny purple berries in fall, prized by birds and wildlife. There is a white form, too.

Buttonbush *(Cephlanthus occidentalis)*   W, S, F, N

Here's a plant with a strong sense of place, and that place is at the margin of any pond, in wetlands and bog gardens. It grows to 15 or more feet if left unpruned and naturally forms a loose mound. This shrub blooms with creamy, ping pong balls of fragrance. The blooms attract bees, then turn to nut brown seed pods in fall and winter favored by waterfowl. I enjoy its rugged, coarse good looks.

Camellia *(C. japonica, C. sasanqua)*   SS, F, E

Choose *sasanqua* for hedging and trees in the shade, *japonica* for focal points. There are so few winter flowering shrubs, yet so relatively few of these make the 'A' list. Go with locally favored varieties and pay for larger specimens when available as they grow slowly but live long garden lives. Acid, fertile and well-drained soils and good sanitation contribute to their success.

Cleyera *(Cleyera japonica)*   D, S, SS, E

Shiny, dark green leaves arranged in whorls give this shrub a decidedly perky attitude. Provide well-drained soil and full sun for thickest form. The steady growth to four to six feet soon develops focal point or hedge plantings, and if left unpruned, cleyera is a good candidate for treeform in less than five years. Use it behind perennials for contrast and as a windbreak.

Eleagnus *(Elaeagnus pungens)*   S, SS, B, E

A good choice for large sites and for making thick mounds of hedging, eleagnus is too often heavily pruned and thus does not flower. That is a great loss in fragrance and nectar for bees. It is a versatile choice with medium green leaves, sometimes with silver lower leaves. Its new growth is coppery in color. It grows rapidly in well-drained soils, slowly but steadily in damp sites.

Fatsia *(Fatsia japonica)*   SS, E

Chubby hand-shaped leaves sprout from scaly trunks that reach five feet in a few years. Fatsia has a coarse texture and tropical attitude, often sporting several shades of green simultaneously as it grows. Reliably hardy to 25 degrees for short periods, it will return from mature roots if frozen down. Well-drained soils in some shade with wind protection works well for it.

Gardenia *(Gardenia jasminoides* and *G. radicans)*
S, SS, F, E

More versatile than my mother's favorite Cape Jasmine, gardenias range from two to eight feet and may be spreading or bushy in form, depending on variety. Some bloom in flushes, others off and on for much of the year. Prune sparingly but regularly after flowering to keep bushes thick. Fertilize when new growth emerges in spring and summer.

Hydrangeas *(Hydrangea macrophylla and other mopheads and lacecaps)* **SS, F**

Childhood was full of these shrubs, four to six feet tall and just as wide, their rounded forms were covered in flowerheads each June. Now there are reblooming (remontant) types, too. On these, the somewhat coarse textured, broad leaves support blooms on both old wood and new. Deadhead to keep new flowers coming until fall. Or leave flowers on the shrubs to mature and cut and hang them to dry as everlastings,

Native Hydrangeas *(Hydrangea arborescens and H. quercifolia)* **S, SS, F**

'Annabelle' is a popular smooth-leaf variety of *H. arborescens* noted for huge, loose flower clusters that change color with age from green to white to tan or brown. Oakleaf hydrangeas (*H. quercifolia*) are noted for conical flower clusters that age from cream to pink and green to tan. mproved varieties boast dense flower clusters that look like mashed potatoes.

Leatherwood *(Cyrilla racemiflora)* 'TiTi' **W, S, SS, F, E, N**

Surely the most macho of native shrubs, aka he-huckleberry, the leatherwood is a wetland native but in time it adapts to conditions almost anywhere. Full sun is favored for garden culture since shady sites lead plants to grow taller than the desired eight feet. Shiny leaves completely cover the canopy all year. It blooms with chains of creamy white flowers, and has nice gnarly bark and trunks. A dry land relative, upland leatherwood (*C. arida*) displays strong drought tolerance.

Loropetalum *(Loropetalum chinensis)* **D, S, SS, F, E**

The classic southern favorite, fringe flower and its more colorful cousins with smaller leaves are sturdy shrubs with fancy tubular flower hats. Varieties range from two to ten feet with flushes of flowers nearly year round. Adapted to any well-drained soil with more abundant flowers in full sun, these are gaining popularity every year but are not yet ubiquitous.

Mahonia *(Mahonia bealei)* **SS, SH, F, B**

Very structured, stiff and spiny like holly, but this shrub adds to its appeal with blue-green leaves, spikes of fragrant yellow flowers, red fall color, and gray-blue berries. Stunning in shade. In a wonderful example of descriptive yet deceptive plant names, mahonia is also called oregon grape holly. It is not any of those things, but resembles the last two a bit.

Nandina *(Nandina domestica)*   D, S, SS, E, B

Almost indestructible, nandina has four season inter-est including bold red winter leaf and fruit color in sun. However, this exotic shrub has escaped and is now considered a pest plant in Florida and should not be planted there. In Zone 8, this is a shrub for hedging, focal point, and container use. Shorter, more colorful varieties do not produce seed nor sucker as much as the species.

Pyracantha *(Pyracantha coccinea)*   S, F, B, E

This rugged fruiting exotic can be used as a focal point plant for its graceful branching, as a dangerously thorny hedge, and as a dramatic espalier on brick walls. Pyracantha will be less prone to fire blight yet grow rapidly and put on berries at a young age if grown without much if any fertilizer. Varieties boast multitudes of berries in red, orange, and yellow.

St. John's Wort *(Hypericum calycinum, H. reductum, H. 'Creels Gold Star')*   S, E, F, N

A tidy leaf habit gives this shrub neat good looks: perfect pairs, longer than wide, pop out opposite each other along stiff stems. Superb yellow summer flowers can resemble pincushions or hairy trumpets, varying in size by cultivar. One or more of the St. Johns worts is adapted to your area, so shop locally for decent drought tolerance and one- to three-foot heights.

Strawberry bush *(Euonymous americanus)*   SS, F, N

A welcome sight in the woods, the strawberry bush is also sold as 'Hearts a Bustin' and 'Wahoo'. It can at first be overlooked in a mixed shrub planting as one more multi-stemmed, light green plant. Its flowers are inconspicuous, but soon become red, dimpled fruits. The 'strawberries' burst open in fall, displaying shiny red seeds at their heart. It is four feet tall and slightly sprawling.

Summersweet *(Clethra alnifolia)*   SS, C, F, N

Grow this shrub for its summer flowers and neat habit in mixed shrub plantings. Clethra's cream-colored flowers appear in fuzzy clusters at the end of each branch with unusual sweetly spicy fragrance. Also called sweet pepperbush, it grows well with azalea, gardenia, and other acid-loving shrubs, and slowly reaches six feet tall if unpruned.

Sweetshrub *(Calycanthus floridus)*   S, SS, SH, F, N

Known as Carolina allspice, strawberry shrub, and even pineapple shrub, the sweetshrub deserves all its nicknames. A vigorous clumper, it soon forms a six- to eight-foot dense thicket in moist shade, creating wildlife cover and nesting places. Control its spread with steel edging to define its space. It is perhaps best known for its spicy maroon flowers in spring and summer.

Sweetspire *(Itea virginica)*   S, SS, F, N

Sweetspire, a shrub three- to five-feet tall and wide with medium green leaves and arching form, is eyecatching year round. Its leaves turn red-purple in fall and may hold on until spring during warm winters. When chains of creamy flowers appear in spring, it is stunning. Though native to damp areas, *Itea* is very adaptable to well-drained organic garden soils.

Wiegela *(Wiegela florida)*   S, SS, F, B

Maintained as thick bundles of canes three to nine feet tall, depending on cultivar, some call wiegela old fashioned, others a cottage garden necessity. Prune these shrubs hard after its masses of tubular spring flowers bloom in order to keep new canes coming, or face die out and fewer flowers in the future. Red fruits keep the wrinkled leaves interesting through fall in sunny sites.

Best Shrubs for Lower Zone 8 and Below

Use in Containers and Protect in Winter Elsewhere

Bottlebrush *(Callistemon citrinus)*   D, S, F

Dense and multi-branched, easily kept to six feet tall, the bottlebrush is the best red shrub, and is softer to touch than it looks. Its red flowers are a hummingbird magnet. Well drained soil is essential.

W-wetland; D-drought tolerant; S-sun preferred; SS-some sun, some shade; SH-shade preferred; E-evergreen; F-flowers; C-fall color; B-berries; N-Southeast native plant.

Ixora, flame-of-the-woods *(Ixora coccinea)*   SS, F

A favorite in morning sun with afternoon shade, flame-of-the-woods blooms in a range of warm hues and thrives in rich, organic soil. Root plants from new growth in spring.

Oleander *(Nerium oleander)*   D, S, F

While technically hardy in Zone 8, oleander suffers in temperatures below 20 degrees F. To avoid damage, protect or containerize it if warranted. All parts are poisonous. It flowers in shades of white, pink, rose, and lavender.

Pittosporum *(Pittosporum tobira)*   S, SS, E

Standard and dwarf types range from 3- 8 and almost as wide. Jade green leaves form into pinwheel arrangements, some edged in white. Spring flowers cluster at stem tips.

Plumbago *(Plumbago auriculata* aka *P. capensis)*   S, SS, E, F

True blue flowers (or white) look like little umbrellas atop light green, soft-looking leaves on this viney shrub. Train the loose stems or let them make mounds of color. It can even be used as a groundcover.

Yesterday today and tomorrow *(Brunfelsia pauciflora)*   SS, F

This three to six foot, open branching shrub is dotted all over with sweet, pansy-looking flowers in spring. They open purple, then age to lavender and finally turn white.

Vines

A nice vine is a delight; an out of control vine is not. Unlike some children and pets, all vines are trainable and benefit mightily from your efforts. The key to a good-looking vine in the garden is finding the right proportion of vine to its support. Tidy clematis can get lost on a vast pergola, perhaps a better home for carolina jessamine or coral honeysuckle. Either of those will soon dwarf the mailbox post that the clematis surrounds perfectly with flowers. Do not underestimate the need to securely anchor trellises and other supports firmly

coral honeysuckle

into the ground. Pour concrete for posts, or pound rebar into the soil and attach metal forms to it for stability. A metal post meant for chicken wire adds spine to fan-shaped wooden trellises. That same rebar can extend the height of short obelisks or become a trellis itself if you know a welder. Get creative and weave a panel trellis to mask a utility box. Just be sure there's room for the vine to reach its heights, and plant the support to stand against the inevitable challenges.

Carolina jessamine *(Gelseminum sempervirens)*   S, SS, F, E

Vigorous, early-blooming native vine with fragrant yellow trumpets will reach 20 feet and is easily trained. Prune after flowering to send new growth where you want it.

Chocolate vine *(Akebia quinata)*   SS, F

A modest vine with neat habits, this one grows steadily to 15 feet. Its blue-purple flowers smell like chocolate. They bloom in spring nestled in sweet whorls of rounded leaflets.

Clematis (several types)   S, SS, F

Shade the roots with mulch or little ground-cover plants and prune as directed: in February cut back those that flower in summer to two buds, chop autumn bloomers way down in spring to control spread, and prune spring bloomers after they flower,

Coral honeysuckle *(Lonicera sempervirens)*   S, SS, E, F

With a medium-fast growth rate to 20 feet, this native honeysuckle features small, tubular red flowers most of the year. It is a hummingbird favorite and a genuinely fine garden plant.

Crossvine *(Bignonia capreolata)*
S, SS, F

This vine will climb to find sunlight, so it is perfect to plant at the base of trees. A true vine in that it climbs with tendrils, crossvine heralds spring with long flower trumpets.

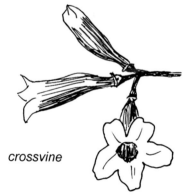

crossvine

Star jasmine *(Trachelospermum jasminoides)* **S, F, E**

Delicious, reliable, hardy, and vigorous if pruned to stimulate new growth, this vine is considered common by some people. Enjoy its fragrance anyway.

Trumpet vine *(Campsis radicans)* **S, SS, F**

Later to bloom than crossvine, this one climbs with aerial roots and blooms later, but equals it for pure flower power. Together, they'll put you on the hummingbird map.

Perennial Flowers, Including Bulbs and Similar Plants

Ajuga *(Ajuga reptans)* **D, SS**

Sweet little blue bugleweed can carpet shady ground for decades and blooms well in even a couple of sunlit hours, attracting beneficial insects. Named varieties offer painted or textured leaves and pink or white flowers.

Angel trumpet *(Brugmansia suaveolens)* **S**

Unbeatable for tropical flair, the leaves and flowers of Brugmansia are commonly more than a foot long. They grow in a wide range of colors on flowers hanging upside down. Note: similar trumpets that point upwards are *Datura*.

Autumn aster *(Aster oblongifolius)* **D, S**

Striking gold centers shoot out lavender ray petals on one- to two-foot upright clumps on this overlooked perennial for wildflower gardens. Cut stems back in fall after flowering.

angel trumpet

Black-eyed Susan *(Rudbeckia hirta, et al)* **D, S**

Yellow daisy-form flowers with flat centers are the standard for hot, dry gardens. A similar effect is achieved with yellow coneflower in wildflower-style borders. Deadheading helps stimulate reblooming.

W-wetland; D-drought tolerant; S-sun preferred; SS-some sun, some shade; SH-shade preferred; E-evergreen; F-flowers; C-fall color; B-berries; N-Southeast native plant.

Boltonia *(Boltonia asteroides)*   D, S, SS

An overlooked native known as snowbank or false aster, boltonia has narrow leaved clumps that burst with nickel-size, white daisies in fall. Cut back in fall after flowering.

Canna *(Canna* species*)*   W, S, SS

Ranging in height from dwarf to tall (three to 12 feet), cannas were confined to the alleys of my childhood. Now, they're prized for their sword-shaped leaves and wild tropical flowers blooming from spring to fall and are featured in many container gardens. Canna leaf roller, a caterpillar, will invade in spring and spoil the leaves if excellent fall sanitation is overlooked.

Canna 'Cleopatra'

Coral bells, Heuchera *(Heuchera americana)*   S, SS, F

Coral bells have been hybridized and popularized so now we have many colors and forms of this native. It flowers on tall spikes and has scalloped rounded leaves that may be green, chartreuse, red, or flashed with silver. It's a grand plant in well-drained soil, in almost full sun, surrounded by creepers like lysimachia.

Daffodil *(Narcissus* species*)* S, SS

Many *Narcissus* varieties naturalize if leaves are allowed to die down after blooming. Prepare a well-drained, organic soil for these long lived bulbs. Plant no deeper than twice the height of the bulb in heavy clay soils.

black-eyed Susan (see left)

Daisy *(Chrysanthemum maximum)* D, S

Shasta daisy types ('Alaska', 'Becky') grow to two feet tall, are multiple-stemmed, and are not invasive. Oxeye native daisies bloom earlier with smaller flowers. For all types, divide their clumps annually.

Daylily *(Hemerocallis* species and hybrids*)* S, SS, some E

Daylilies are indispensable for their easy exuberance, though not good for cutting since each flower lasts but one day, closing up by dinner time. That said, plant groups of daylilies in sunny beds for strong garden style and blooms that go on for many weeks in summer. Separate old-fashioned sorts ('Kwanso' and my mother's favorite 'Golden Gift') from newer varieties. The old gals were meant to spread and fill a bed or bank, while the poly and tetraploids are meant to occupy their own space. Some new hybrids go dormant, some don't; some rebloom, some don't. Shop locally, at least at first. If you can visit a local breeder by all means do so.

Dianthus *(Dianthus* species and hybrids*)* SS

Neat, blue-gray pincushion of leaves paired with clove-scented, fringed spring flowers make a bridge between the other pinks and the sweet William types. The former are reliably perennial in well-drained soil; the latter are grown as overwintering annuals.

Gladiola (*Gladiolus*)

Start planting corms in February and continue weekly through March for flowers from late April through Father's Day. Stake when planting and cut when the first flowers open but the top of the stalk is still in bud.

Grape hyacinth *(Muscari* species*)* S, SS

Grape hyacinths are small bulbs with big impact. Just six inches tall, their small purple flower spikes top neat foliage clumps to make a fine skirt to tulips or snapdragons, or look great when massed by themselves. Woods hyacinth and other relatives are nice too, but in our climate grape hyacinth is easier to keep going for several years.

Iris *(many species)*   S, SS

A huge family with more cousins every year, *Iris* species are divided into two distinct categories: bearded and beardless. The beard is a fuzzy line that runs  down the petals that hang down (falls). The upright petals are called standards. Beardless iris are clean-shaven and have different petal arrangements than the classic bearded type. Except for the Louisianas and fulvas, iris demand great drainage to thrive and multiply. This applies to both traditional rhizomes and the bulbous types known as Dutch iris. All are considered heavy feeders, but excess nitrogen, especially manure, can contribute to rhizome rot.

Bearded iris are fussy and fabulous. Full sun and great drainage are essential, so consider raised beds or rows within beds. Amend heavy soils with ground barks and compost. Plant shallowly, and do not mulch over the tops of rhizomes, which show above ground.

Favorite Beardless Iris

Louisianas and their parent, copper iris, thrive in ditches and bogs, but can adapt to most garden soils with moderate amounts of irrigation. They bloom late and begin new growth in September. Do not cut them for indoor arrangements because the odor resembles cat urine.

Crested iris have long leaves near ground level that look like fans laid down and forgotten. The genteel flowers are ruffled white with delicate yellow and purple markings. These are said to be a slug favorite, but not in a well-drained raised bed.

Yellow and blue flags offer the tallest leaves and fattest rhizomes. They make very strong design statements even when grown in shade too dense for flowering. The blues are native to the south, and are reputed to have been used by Seminoles to treat victims of alligator bites! Yellows are invasive in aquatic environments but easily controlled on dry land.

***Iris* spuria** types are limited to very, very well drained soil, but bloom later than beardeds. They have taller, sharper leaves and tighter flower arrangements; they're good for cutting.

Siberians have stiff narrow leaves for a very neat garden appearance, growing to three feet tall depending on selection. The flowers curl sweetly down at edges, and despite their name, are fine for much of the South when grown in afternoon shade.

Others

Japanese iris display fat flowers, that is, wide falls with silky texture and short, tight standards. **Miniature bearded iris** are a group unto themselves, needing nearly pure gravel planting medium to avoid rot. Not truly an iris, **Fortnight lily**

(Dietes) deserves attention in the warmest areas for its similar look and great garden performance. Some people call it African iris.

Lantana *(Lantana camara)*   D, S

If you can only have one nectar plant for butterflies in a hot, dry spot, this is it. Get a splash of water under the leaves regularly to prevent summer's spider mites. Plant only sterile, nonfruiting varieties in public areas, and be aware that this plant is toxic to people and livestock. It is also considered invasive and not to be planted at all in Florida.

Lamb's Ears *(Stachys byzantina)*   D, S, SS

Fuzzy, gray leaves in low-growing clumps eventually bring on this plant's yellow flower spikes. But cut them off soon after they appear to keep the leaves growing and new clumps coming.

Lily (*Lilium* species)

Not grown as widely as they could be, tiger lily and her friends bring drama to late spring. Tuck a bulb or ten into a sunny, well-drained bed amid other perennials or shrubs. Stake if needed and pick for the vase.

Phlox *(Phlox divaricata, P. paniculata 'Robert Poore', P. subulata)* S, SS

There's wild blue phlox but also pink and downright purplish *P. divaricata*. This species flowers early in part shade, and spreads nicely in rich soil. 'Robert Poore' resists powdery mildew and reaches three or more feet tall. Its upright, purple-pink flowers resemble the color of the dated, mildew-ridden phlox. *P. subulata* or creeping phlox is known best for hugging the ground with needle-like leaves and riotous pink flowers in early spring. Variations exist on all of these that are worth trying, and yes, *P. drummondii* does ok for annual planting.

130

Reseeders I Love

Mexican hat (Ratibida columnaris) and candelabra plant (Senna alata) represent the best of reseeding annuals. Resilient in the summer heat, the hats drop seeds to keep their clump fresh for years in dry, very well-drained soils. It is excellent to establish along driveways and hot spots near streets. Aka candle tree or candlestick bush, Senna seeds are collected at first frost, tossed in a drawer, and started in January for spring planting. Reliably lovely in the garden, it is equally reliable from saved seed.

Purple coneflower (Echinacea purpurea) S, SS

Large daisy-shaped flowers with pointed centers grow lavishly on plants to two feet tall with fuzzy green leaves. White varieties are less vigorous than the usual pink ones, but lovely. New echinaceas in yellow tones have been introduced.

Red hot poker *(Kniphofia* species and hybrids*)* D, S

These sharp-looking, skinny upright leaf clumps are foolproof in hot, dry settings. Stalks of spiky orange and yellow blooms contrast with everything else in the spring garden.

Sedum, stonecrop (*Sedum* species and hybrids) D, S

Lots of stonecrops are a joy in the garden, from showy sedum to hen and chicks and dragonsblood, but *Sedum* 'Autumn Joy' is the most reliable. Two-foot tall, waxy light green stems and round leaves, this one has starry white flower clusters that turn mahogany by fall.

Spider lilies *(Lycoris radiata, L. squamigia, L. lutea)* D, S, SS

Red spiders, hurricane lilies, and golden spiders bloom in fall, clumps of leaves follow. The reds haunt old home sites, usually marking paths and driveways. Mark the clump, then transplant when the leaves have died back in late spring.

Spiderworts *(Tradescantia x andersoniana)* SS, S

Common on roadsides, both blue and pink types deserve a spot in your garden. In poor soil or good, grow them with wild violets and wild strawberries in an overlooked spot. The blue is rampant, the pink much neater in habit.

Stokes aster *(Stokesia laevis)* D, S, SS

Neat clumps stay low to the ground, giving this plant a bright spot in the front of any border. Bold purple-blue, pink, and white pincushion-shaped blooms stand up on sturdy stems, unwilted by heat.

Summer snowflake, snowdrop *(Leucojum aestivum)* S, SS

Leucojum is called summer snowflake. The true snowdrop is *Galanthus* and is not a good choice for us. Plant snowflakes in fall with the other Dutch bulbs for one-foot tall clumps of strappy leaves and cup-shaped flowers with characteristic tiny green dots on each lip. These are beautiful and indestructible.

Trillium *(Trillium cuneatum)*   SS

Known as sweet Betsy or toadshade, trillium is a woodland native right at home in shady gardens; its low-growing stands of mottled leaves are topped by purple flowers in spring.

White spider lily *(Hymenocallis* species*)* W, SS

Native bulb with strappy blade-shaped leaves, wild white pinwheel flowers in late spring and summer. Adaptable to good garden soil with regular water.

Foliage

Not so much for their flowers, these perennials are grown for spectacular leaves:

Caladium   *(Caladium   bicolor)* SS, SH

and Dahlia *(D. spp.)*   S, F

These are the only two bulblike plants I love that are worth all the trouble. Even where they are hardy, both will be more successful if dug and stored over winter because of the rots associated with heavy, wet soils.

W-wetland; D-drought tolerant; S-sun preferred; SS-some sun, some shade; SH-shade preferred; E-evergreen; F-flowers; C-fall color; B-berries; N-Southeast native plant.

Castor bean *(Ricinus communis)*   S, SS

Stunning red leaves and stems in full sun would be enough, but the rough texture and huge sized leaves are rivaled only by rice paper plant for fast tropical attitude. Poisonous.

Elephant ears *(Alocasia* and *Colocasia* species)   SS

Alocasia leaves stand mostly upright, Colocasia faces down, and between these species, they have the territory covered from huge heart-shapes in lime green to almost black.

Ornamental Grasses

Miscanthus group *(Miscanthus sinensis et al.)* includes the species, considered invasive in some places (check before you plant), maiden grass thought best for the warmest areas, stiff variegated porcupine grass, and silver feather, perhaps best overall.

Mondo grass *(Ophiopogon japonicus)* is not a true grass but its use and care are similar. Cut back in late winter, though not as radically.

Muhly grass *(Muhlenbergia lindheimeri)* is native to Texas, but well-adapted elsewhere in sunny gardens. Flower spikes are dense and 'Autumn Glow' looks like cotton candy.

Ferns

True ferns number an amazing 12,000, around the globe, so it is possible your favorite one is not included in this group. These are the ones I like best, and at least two of the four will grow easily for you.

Autumn fern *(Dryopteris erythrosora)* **SS, SH, E**

Small with a neat habit, the autumn fern keeps its place at two by two feet. Its coppery new growth turns green, then rusty brown even in damp soils, adding needed contrast to shady beds.

Christmas fern *(Polystichum acrostichoides)* **SS, SH, E**

Christmas is an evergreen native fern two to three feet tall and wide. It offers leathery fronds in strongly upright form. Usually the greenest plant in the winter woodland, it is popular for holiday decorating.

Holly fern *(Crytomium falcatum)* **D, SS, SH, E**

About three by three feet, this coarse-textured fern survives in dry shade, but thrives with minimal watering. Although it is reputed to be resistant to deer, a thirsty deer doesn't resist anything much.

Southern shield *(Thelypteris kunthii)* **SS, SH**

This native fern grows to three feet tall and even wider, with lime-green prehistoric-looking fronds. It spreads fast in acid soil. People love it or they hate it. I'm a huge fan.

Hardy Palms

To 0 degrees:

Needle palm *(Rhapidophyllum hystrix)* Warm walls and microclimates can extend the range of needle palm through nearly all of the deep south. The fronds are finely cut, thus its name, and though native to the hardwood forest understory, needle palm is flexible. Grown in shade or full sun, it is drought tolerant after a couple of years in the ground. Needle palm slowly reaches five feet tall and forms a bold, wide cluster from ground level with no trunk.

To 5 degrees:

Windmill palm *(Tracycarpus fortunei)* Aka Chinese fan or Chusan, windmill palm boasts the classic profile of trunk topped by fronds on a 30 foot tree. It can adapt to all but the boggiest gardens, but partly shady sites are preferred to maintain its light green and silvery fronds.

Mediterranean fan palm *(Chamaerops humilis)* Native to Europe, this fan palm is a happy import. Relatively small fronds burst from slow growing trunks that eventually reach 15 feet tall with three-sided leaves. Each is two feet square and very segmented. This palm suffers in very wet or very dry sites.

To 15 degrees:

Pindo or jelly palm *(Butia capitata)* You can, indeed, make delicious jelly with the abundant fruit of this palm. But if left on the tree, it rots and attracts a riot of insects. Strong trunk and feathery, upright fronds make pindo palm a lovely landscape plant. Drought tolerant and especially lovely in some shade, pindo prefers sandy soil but can adapt to any well-drained site.

Dwarf palmetto *(Sabal minor)* Seek out local adapted dwarf palms for even greater cold tolerance than the species. Also called blue stem and blue palm, dwarf palmetto keeps its trunk underground and sends up fronds from 2 to 5 feet tall. Best grown ala its native environment in damp woodlands, dwarf palm will adapt to more sunlight and less water over time.

Sago palm (Cycas revoluta) is a cycad, one of the garden's living fossils going back to the age of dinosaurs. They resemble palms more than anything else and, like most palms, prefer bright light and ample water in well drained soil. Male and female plants add strong tropical character well into zone 8. With similar protection, sago palm can rival needle palm for hardiness. It will lose fronds and some will turn tan, but the plant will survive and resprout after challenging winters.

dwarf palmetto

<u>Notes</u>

Reading list

For in-depth information about specific topics addressed in this book, consult these references. Some of them are new, a few very old and perhaps only available from used book dealers. In a library of more than 200 garden books, these stay closest at hand.

Teaming with Microbes: A Gardener's Guide to the Soil Food Web by Jeff Lowenfels and Wayne Lewis, 2006, Timber Press, Portland, OR.

Gardening in the Humid South by Edmund N. O'Rourke, Jr., and Leon C. Standifer, 2002, LSU Press, Baton Rouge, LA.

Creative Propagation by Peter Thompson, 2005, Timber Press, Portland, OR.

The Gardener's A-Z Guide to Growing Flowers from Seed to Bloom by Eileen Powell, 2004, Storey Books, North Adams, MA.

Step by Step Organic Vegetable Gardening by Shepherd Ogden, 1992, Harper-Collins Books, New York, NY.

Grow Organic by Doug Oster and Jessica Walliser, 2007, St. Lynn's Press, Pittsburgh, PA.

Good Bug, Bad Bug by Jessica Walliser, 2008, St. Lynn's Press, Pittsburgh, PA.

The Pruning Book by Lee Reich, 1999 (hardback, 1997), Taunton Press, Newtown, CT.

Southern Herb Growing by Madeline Hill and Gwen Barkley, 1987, Shearer Publishing, Fredricksburg, TX.

The Southern Kitchen Garden by William Adams and Thomas Leroy, 2007, Taylor Trade Publishing, Lanham, MD.

Bulletproof Flowers for the South by Jim Wilson, 1999, Taylor Publishing, Dallas, TX.

Garden Perennials for the Coastal South by Barbara Sullivan, 2003, UNC Press, Chapel Hill, NC.

Native Perennials for the Southeast by Peter Loewer, 2004, Cool Springs Press, Nashville, TN.

The Gardener's Book of Lists by Lois Trigg Chapin, 1994, Taylor Publishing, Dallas, TX.

Encyclopedia of Organic Gardening by Rodale Press staff and editors, 1999 edit., Emmaus, PA.

Dirr's Trees and Shrubs for Warm Climates by Michael Dirr, 2002, Timber Press, Portland, OR.

Identification, Selection, and Use of Southern Plants by Neil Odenwald and James Turner, 1996 edit., Claitor's Publishing Division, Baton Rouge, LA.

Armitage's Manual of Annuals, Biennials, and Half Hardy Perennials by Allan Armitage, 2001, Timber Press, Portland, OR.

Southern Living Garden Book edited by Steve Bender, Oxmoor House, Birmingham, AL.

And for inspiration anytime.... *Chicken Soup for the Gardener's Soul* edited by Pat Stone et al, 2000, Health Communications, Inc., Deerfield Beach, FL. And don't forget to look at *GreenPrints* ("The Weeder's Digest"), P. O. Box 1355, Fairview, NC 28730.

More Resources

If I tried to list everything else that is helpful in gardening, I would surely leave something out, but there are a few venues you shouldn't miss. First are newspaper columnists who communicate regularly with local gardeners. Two in particular are decidedly unSouthern but deserve a read when you run into them online: Irene Virag and Ann Lovejoy never fail to teach me something in five hundred to a thousand words.

Individual state gardening guides and magazines are valuable for local calendars of events and planting dates, as well as information from your state's Cooperative Extension Service.

Websites to bookmark include:

gardenmama.com (of course!)

floridata.com

longcreekherbs.com

arborday.org

reneesgardenseeds.com

brentandbeckysbulbs.com

kitazawaseed.com

gardenrant.com

themulch.com

whatsthatbug.com

nationalgardening.com

and all local websites such as newspapers with a gardening page.

Index

141

More Great Garden Books from
B. B. Mackey Books
P. O. Box 475, Wayne, PA 19087

B. B. Mackey Books is an award-winning publisher of garden books on special subjects. Find out details and order online from **www.mackeybooks.com**. Or ask for these titles from **www.Amazon.com** or a full-service bookseller in your area.

To order by mail, copy this list and include payment by check. Add $2 for shipping of any order. If you are ordering from Pennsylvania, add 6 percent state sales tax.

___***Creating & Planting Alpine Gardens,*** by Rex Murfitt, Softcover, 276 pages. Garden Writers Association award 2006. **$ 22.50.**

___***Creating & Planting Garden Troughs,*** by Fingerut and Murfitt. How to do it! American Horticultural Society book award 2000. Hardcover, 178 pages. **$21.00.**

___***A Cutting Garden for Florida,*** by Mackey and Brandies. Grow it in Florida! Condition like a pro. Softcover, 141 pages. **$15.95**

___***Florida Gardening: the Newcomers Survival Manual, 2nd Ed,*** by Monica Brandies. Great advice coaches you through! Softcover, 136 pages. **$19.95.**

___***Garden Notes Through the Years*** (4-year blank journal) designed by Betty Mackey for your notes. Synchronize your flower borders! Softcover, lay-flat binding. 112 pages. **$11.95.**

___***Herbs and Spices for Florida Gardens,*** by Monica Brandies. How to use and grow flavorful and useful plants. Softcover, 246 pages. **$15.50.**

___**Organic Gardening Down South,** by Nellie Neal. Softcover, 143 pages. **$15.95.**

___***Questions & Answers for Deep South Gardeners,*** by Nellie Neal. Gardenmama answers everyone's garden questions. Softcover, 120 pages. **$12.95.** New edition pending (2009).

___***Who Does Your Garden Grow,*** by Alex Pankhurst. Paperback reprint of the British book. Fascinating stories of people and plants. Softcover, 146 pages. **$15.95.**

~~~

Over time, prices and availability may change and new editions and new titles will be added.

For wholesale orders for stores or garden clubs inquire at info@mackeybooks.com.

Printed in the United States
216252BV00004B/1/P

9 781893 443105